Guidebook on

LANDFIRE Fuels Data Acquisition, Critique, Modification, Maintenance, and Model Calibration

Richard D. Stratton

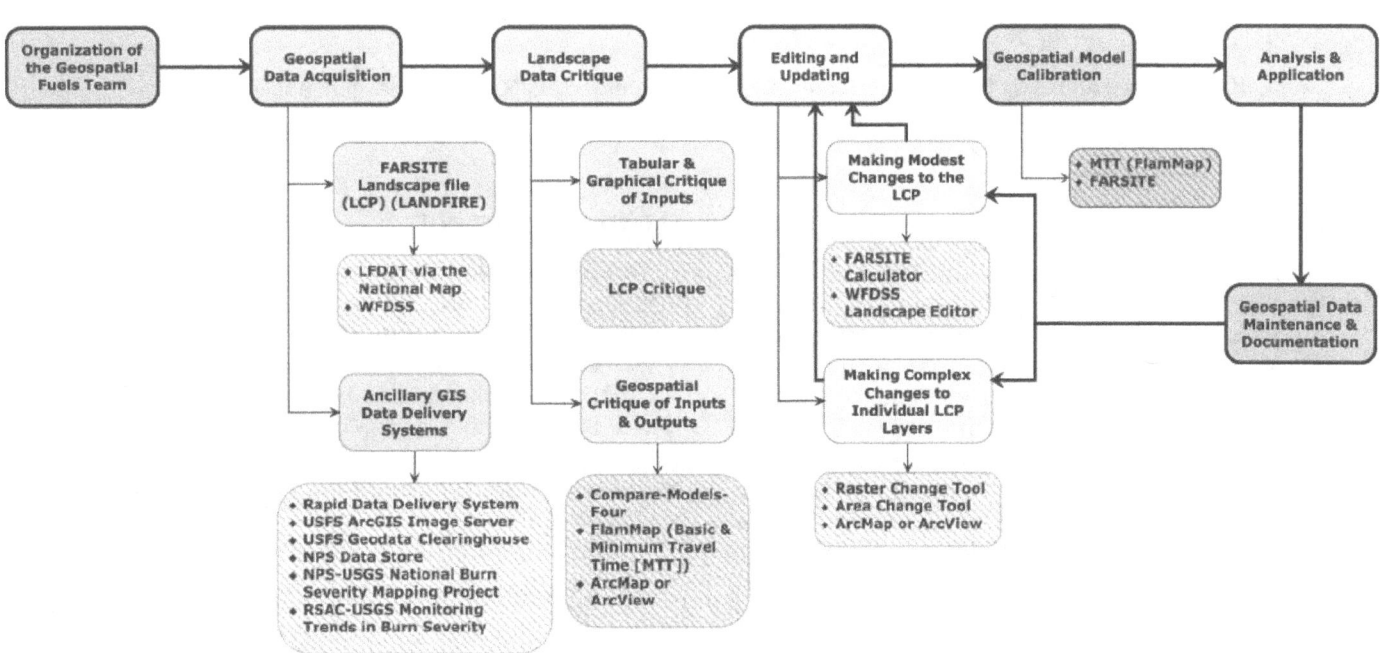

 USDA United States Department of Agriculture

Forest Service

Rocky Mountain Research Station

General Technical Report RMRS-GTR-220

February 2009

Stratton, Richard D. 2009. **Guidebook on LANDFIRE fuels data acquisition, critique, modification, maintenance, and model calibration**. Gen. Tech. Rep. RMRS-GTR-220. Fort Collins, CO: U.S. Department of Agriculture, Forest Service, Rocky Mountain Research Station. 54 p.

Abstract

With the advent of LANDFIRE fuels layers, an increasing number of specialists are using the data in a variety of fire modeling systems. However, a comprehensive guide on acquiring, critiquing, and editing (ACE) geospatial fuels data does not exist. This paper provides guidance on ACE as well as on assembling a geospatial fuels team, model calibration, and maintaining geospatial data and documentation.

The LANDFIRE Data Access Tool (LFDAT), an ArcMap extension, and the Wildland Fire Decision Support System (WFDSS) are the primary tools outlined in this guide to obtain the Fire Area Simulator (FARSITE) landscape file (LCP) for geospatial fuels application. Other useful geographic information system (GIS) data acquisition websites and layers for geospatial fire analysis are also provided. Critiquing the data consists of (1) a tabular critique of the inputs using LCP Critique and (2) a geospatial critique of the inputs and outputs using FlamMap and ArcMap. Detailed information is provided on many of the layers that constitute the LCP (fuel model, canopy cover, stand height, crown base height, crown bulk density).

Inputs are spatially critiqued using FlamMap and ArcMap in combination with the existing vegetation type layer. Outputs critiqued include flame length, rate of spread, fireline intensity, crown fire activity, and fire growth. Compare-Models-Four and Minimum Travel Time (MTT) are discussed, the WFDSS landscape editor is demonstrated as a tool to edit and update an LCP and a section on model calibration using FARSITE and MTT is included. The paper concludes with direction and discussion on data maintenance, documentation, and complexities of a national fuels dataset for field application.

Keywords: FARSITE, fire behavior, fire modeling, FlamMap, GIS, geospatial fire analysis, LCP Critique, LFDAT, MTT, WFDSS

Author Profile

Richard D. Stratton is a fire modeling analyst with Systems for Environmental Management (SEM), a research, development, and education organization located in Missoula, Montana. His research interests include geospatial fire modeling, wildland fire use, fuel treatment design, hazard and risk assessment, and home ignitability from wildland fires. Rick received his B.S. degree in conservation biology from Brigham Young University and his M.S. degree in forestry (fire and GIS emphasis) from Utah State University. Previous to SEM, he worked eight seasons with the U.S. Forest Service/National Park Service in various biological and fire suppression and monitoring capacities.

Acknowledgments

This document was funded by the National Park Service and supported by LANDFIRE and the U.S. Forest Service, Rocky Mountain Research Station, Missoula Fire Sciences Laboratory, Fire Modeling Institute, and Wildland Fire RD&A. I acknowledge helpful reviews from Joe Scott, Laurie Kurth, Chuck McHugh, Pat Stephen, and Tobin Kelley. I also express my thanks to Kristi Coughlon for editorial assistance and Nancy Chadwick for page composition.

Contents

Introduction

In the past, the main limiting factor to geospatial fire modeling was the lack of data. Fire Area Simulator (FARSITE) (Finney 1998) landscape file (LCP) development was limited to geographic areas with the expertise, financial support, and need (e.g., large land-base) for fire modeling. This created a haphazard patchwork of LCPs for fire and fuel management specialists and analysts (hereafter referred to as *fire specialists*) to use. With the arrival of LANDFIRE (www.landfire.gov), a nationwide fire, fuel, and vegetation mapping project that provides nationally consistent and seamless products (including FARSITE layers), data availability is no longer an issue. However, there is an increased need for data evaluation, reprojection, modification, and maintenance. LANDFIRE National data, as well as any other geospatial dataset, must be critiqued, edited, updated, and maintained to yield "accurate" information. Unfortunately, inadequate organizational support exists at the field level and limited training or instruction has been given on management of geospatial fuels data.

This paper is a "how to" guide for acquiring, critiquing, and editing (ACE) LANDFIRE fuels data. It also provides guidance on assembling a fuels team, calibration of spatial fire growth models, and maintaining geospatial data and documentation (fig. 1). *An abbreviation and acronym list is provided in Appendix A.*

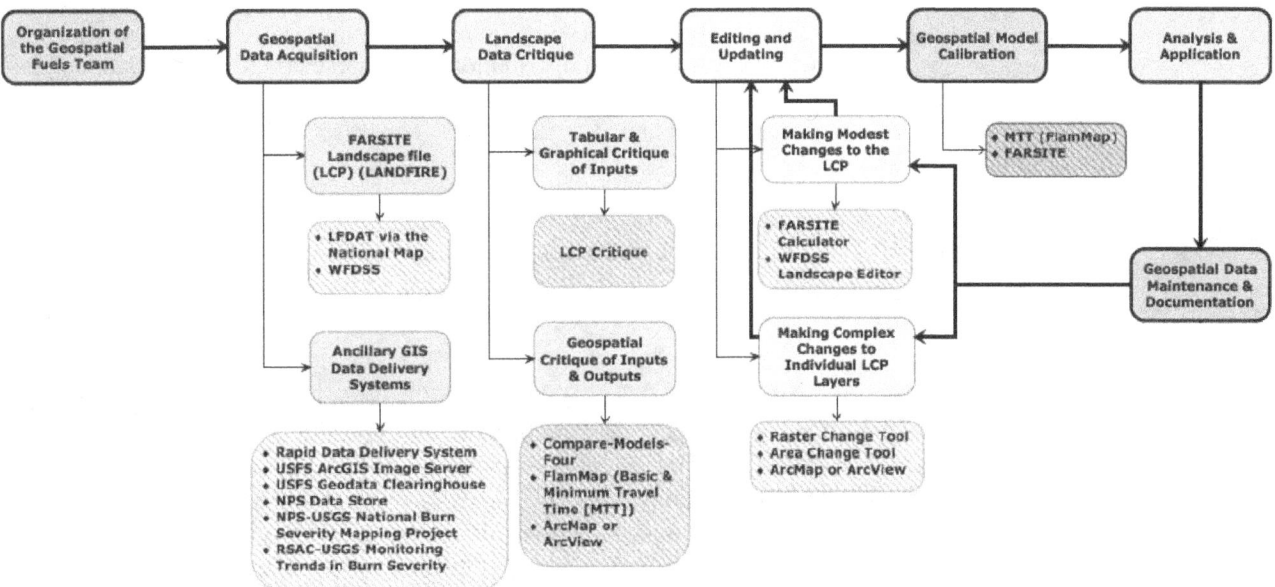

Figure 1. Flow chart of the "life cycle" of geospatial fuels data. The thick line delineates the main process flow. Programs and modeling/information systems are displayed with a hatch.

USDA Forest Service Gen. Tech. Rep. RMRS-GTR-220. 2009

1

The Geospatial Fuels Team

In the past, FARSITE LCPs were critiqued, edited, and updated, and models were calibrated in three ways: using groups, individuals, or a combination of the two. With the group approach, a team of experts is assembled in a workshop setting and systematically works through the analysis (Bahro and others 2007). The individual approach requires a fire specialist to take on the process alone and produce a product (Stratton 2004). From experience, a combination of the two approaches is most effective. It is best that a fire modeling analyst or savvy fuels specialist take the lead in facilitating and accomplishing most of the work. However, including others in the decision making process creates better fuels data and collaborators are more apt to use and recommend the product.

Selecting the right individuals with the appropriate level of fire behavior and modeling experience and adequate local knowledge is critical to a successful outcome. If you get too many, you become overwhelmed with opinions; too few, and important information is missed. Also, consider including personnel from adjoining areas (e.g., fire planning unit [FPU]) or those that have gone through a comparable process in similar terrain and fuel. The analysis team should be composed of individuals:

- that have observed fires locally in various fuel and weather conditions for many years (e.g., fire management officer [FMO], assistant FMO [AFMO], fire behavior analyst [FBAN]);
- with geospatial fire modeling experience to help bridge the gap between field observations and the modeling systems (e.g., long-term analyst [LTAN], fuels specialist);
- familiar with vegetation type, distribution, and characteristics (e.g., stand heights) (e.g., forester, silviculturalist, ecologist, botanist); and
- with geographic information system (GIS) expertise, particularly in grid (raster) analysis.

Geospatial Data Acquisition

The FARSITE Landscape File

There are several ways to obtain geospatial data for fire modeling. The most common data format for geospatial fire analysis is the FARSITE/FlamMap LCP, a single binary file consisting of elevation, slope, aspect, fuel model (see Anderson 1982; Scott and Burgan 2005), and canopy cover (CC) – required inputs – as well as optional themes of stand height (SH), crown base height (CBH), canopy bulk density (CBD), duff loading, and coarse woody debris (Finney 1998) (fig. 2). Duff loading and coarse woody debris layers – not available from LANDFIRE – are used by the post-frontal combustion model, which permits calculations of heat flux and emissions used to estimate smoke production and soil heating. A standard practice is to create an LCP using the five required files and the three canopy characteristic files. Development of the optional themes may not be necessary in areas where crown fire spread is of little concern (e.g., hardwood forests). The LCP is built by importing each theme as an ASCII Raster – a common file format for an exported GIS layer.

LANDFIRE LCP themes are available on DVD from the Remote Sensing Application Center (RSAC) (http://www.fs.fed.us/eng/rsac), from the National Map (http://landfire.cr.usgs.gov/viewer), or from the Wildland Fire Decision Support System (WFDSS) (http://wfdss.nwcg.gov).

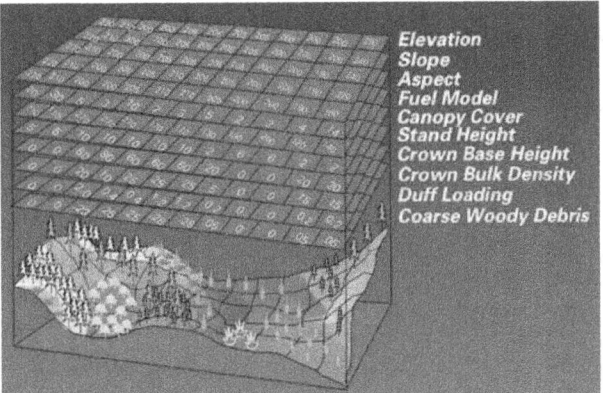

Figure 2. FARSITE landscape file or LCP "sandwich" (courtesy of Mark Finney).

Downloading LANDFIRE Data Using LFDAT

The LANDFIRE Data Access Tool (LFDAT) (version 2.0) is an ArcGIS toolbar developed by the U.S. Forest Service (USFS), Rocky Mountain Research Station (RMRS) and distributed by the National Interagency Fuels Technology Team (NIFTT). This tool enables users to interactively download LANDFIRE data from the National Map LANDFIRE data server *within* ArcMap (version 9.0-9.3) as zipped files in either Environmental System Research Institute (ESRI) ArcGRID or GeoTiff format. The program also allows users to batch unzip, assemble, and reproject downloaded layers, as well as build and dissemble an LCP. Both LANDFIRE National and Rapid Refresh data are available for download.

(1) Download LFDAT from the LANDFIRE website and install the program (http://www.landfire.gov/products_tools.php). A comprehensive tutorial is available at www.niftt.gov; click on **Tools and User Documents** to download (optional).

(2) Open ArcMap and locate the newly installed LFDAT toolbar (fig. 3). If it is not visible, you may need to manually select the toolbar to display (**Tools > Customize…**, select LANDFIRE Data Access Tool). Click the paperclip to **Check for updates** to the National Map and view the User Guide. Click on **Add Layer Showing LANDFIRE Data Availability** (two yellow rectangles with a down arrow). A United States map with LANDFIRE map zones will be displayed.

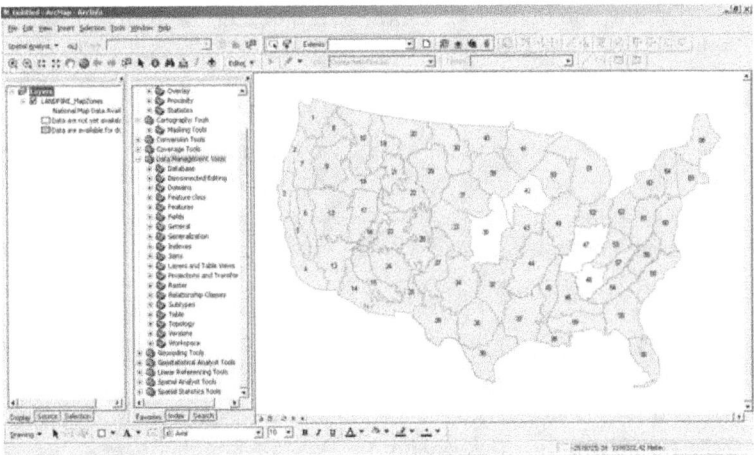

Figure 3. The LFDAT tool bar (framed in red) and a view of the LANDFIRE zones in ArcMap available via LFDAT. Areas in light green are complete and available for download.

USDA Forest Service Gen. Tech. Rep. RMRS-GTR-220. 2009

3

(3) Click **Get LANDFIRE National Map Data** (red dashed rectangle). Move your mouse to the upper left corner of the area you are interested in extracting, left click, then drag the box to the lower right corner. A download window will appear. Name your clip boundary in the **Save this extent** box. Select **Google-map this** to open a web browser with the extraction box displayed in Google Maps. You may want to save a screen capture of this image.

(4) Go back to the download window and click the dropdown arrow to reveal the LAND-FIRE layers available for download. Download the FARSITE layers in table 1 by selecting the layer, clicking **Request Download**, and clicking **Download** on the request summary page to initiate the extraction process. Also, download the existing vegetation type (EVT) layer.

Table 1. LANDFIRE FARSITE layer units.

LANDFIRE layer	Units
Elevation	meters
Slope	degrees
Aspect	azimuth degrees
Fuel model	n/a
Canopy cover	percent
Canopy height	meters, * 10
Canopy base height	meters, * 10
Canopy bulk density	kg/m^3, *100

When the extraction is complete, a window appears. Select **Save**, choose the file location, and click **Save**. The extraction process takes a couple of minutes, but the download process varies greatly depending on your internet connection and the size of the area you delineated. Also, sometimes files become corrupt when downloading, requiring a second try, so don't close out of ArcMap.

Unzipping, Merging, and Reprojecting LANDFIRE Data Using LFDAT

LANDFIRE data extracted from the National Map needs to be unzipped, renamed, assembled, and reprojected (all GIS data is in an Albers projection). A map projection is a mathematical calculation to portray all or part of the earth on a flat surface. The Albers equal-area conic projection is commonly used for the continental United States or other large land bases, often running east-west (United States Geological Survey [USGS] 2000). Your local area (e.g., Forest) will likely use a different coordinate system (e.g., UTM [projection] NAD 83 [Datum]) and you will want to reproject the LANDFIRE data to the local projection to minimize error and enable local GIS data overlays.

LFDAT has automated the process of unzipping, renaming, assembling, and reprojecting the LANDFIRE data. Files extracted from the National Map are given an 8-digit random number that is changed to a recognizable name (e.g., slope_1). Also, depending on the size of the area extracted, the layer may be divided into "pieces" that need to be merged back together. When all of the layers are downloaded, click **Process and Assemble LANDFIRE National Map data** located on the LFDAT toolbar. In a few seconds, the LANDFIRE Smart Assembler window will be displayed. Select the folder where the FARSITE files reside, create a new folder (e.g., LCP_UTM_NAD83), choose ESRI GRID for output type, select the output projection (e.g., If your local unit uses UTM, select **Projected Coordinate Systems** and the appropriate zone, or select an existing projection file [.prj], or import an existing raster or vector layer), save the projection/coordinate system information to your new folder (creates a .prj file), click **Assemble Data**. When the process is complete, text at the bottom of the window will state "Processing done in * minutes." Close the assembler window by clicking the "**X**" in the upper right.

Building an LCP File Using LFDAT

An LCP can be built once the FARSITE data has been assembled and reprojected (if needed). Click **LFDAT Raster Utilities** (Swiss Army Knife) on the toolbar and **Build LCP File**. Click the down arrow for each layer to establish a file path to the proper grid. The default units and latitude should be correct, but double-check with table 1. Specify a name for the LCP and click **Build LCP**. Click **OK** when the program has completed building the LCP. Close the Build LCP window.

Downloading an LCP Using WFDSS

An alternative to the National Map is WFDSS. This system was designed to assist land managers and fire specialists in determining the appropriate management response (AMR) on fire incidents. WFDSS is under development; updates and enhancements to the system are being made regularly. For that reason, a step-by-step process is not outlined. Currently, the only way to download an LCP is to (1) log into the system, (2) create an incident, (3) request an FSPro analysis, (4) define the LCP extent, and (5) download the LCP. Because WFDSS was not intended to be a dissemination site for LANDFIRE data, this process is convoluted, but can be quicker than the National Map, particularly when downloading a large area. It also allows users to download *an LCP* instead of individual layers that need to be assembled and an LCP constructed. Although there is no way to reproject the LCP data using WFDSS, you could use the LFDAT tool to disassemble the WFDSS generated LCP, reproject the layers into a local projection (ArcMap), and reassemble the LCP. Future enhancements to WFDSS may include reprojection and easier LCP download.

Obtaining Ancillary GIS Data

Before the LCP and fire behavior outputs can be critiqued, it is important to gather GIS reference and analysis layers. A list of some of the most useful data is provided below (table 2).

Table 2. List of GIS layers for fuels critique, modification, and model calibration.

Disturbance History
Burn severity
Fire progression
Fuel treatments
Insect and disease
Prescribed fire perimeters
Storm damage (e.g., blow down, hurricane)
Wildfire perimeters

Ecological Considerations
Rivers and streams
Water bodies

Socio-Economic Considerations
Ownership & jurisdiction
Historical and recreational sites
Primary and secondary residences
Remote Automated Weather Stations (RAWS)
Roads
Trails
Urban development

Other Base Layers
Aerial photos
Digital orthophoto quad (DOQ) or quarter quad (DOQQ)
Digital raster graph (DRG)
Vegetation or cover-type classification

USDA Forest Service Gen. Tech. Rep. RMRS-GTR-220. 2009

5

Landscape modifications and disturbance information is critical. LANDFIRE national data products are based on NLCD (National Land Cover Data) imagery circa 2001. The LAND-FIRE Rapid Refresh dataset used principally fire perimeters and burn severity to account for recent disturbances, but it is important that recent disturbances are verified. Consider making a list of all natural or human-made landscape disturbances that need to be accounted for in the LCP. Some of these may include wildfires, prescribed fires, mechanical fuel treatments, harvested stands, beetle-killed stands, and storm damage.

United States Geological Survey Rapid Data Delivery System (RDDS) (http://firedata.cr.usgs.gov)

- This is a very functional, efficient, and reliable system used to obtain geospatial information. A user can zoom to an area of interest or select **Quick Find** to view a fire location, define an area to extract, select products, specify a projection, and download the data. Products include vector and raster data such as active and previous fires, moderate resolution imaging spectroradiometer (MODIS), remote automated weather stations (RAWS), roads, rivers, lakes, ownership, orthoimagery, DRGs, and digital elevation models (DEM) (fig. 4). A login is needed to access the site and is easily obtained.

USFS ArcGIS Image Server (http://fsweb.rsac.fs.fed.us/imageserver/imageserver.html)

- Using ArcGIS Image Server, an extension to ArcGIS (version 9.1 and 9.2), RSAC and the Geospatial Service and Technology Center (GSTC) have compiled imagery of the United States accessible to all *USFS computers* via ArcMap (fig. 5). Available imagery includes high resolution orthophotography, Landsat TM (15 m), km MODIS (1 km), topographic maps (1:24 k, 1:100 k, and 1:250 k), and shaded relief maps (10 m-1 km). There are easy to follow installation instructions and a tutorial at http://fsweb.geotraining.fs.fed.us. A high-speed internet connection is crucial for efficient use of the utility.

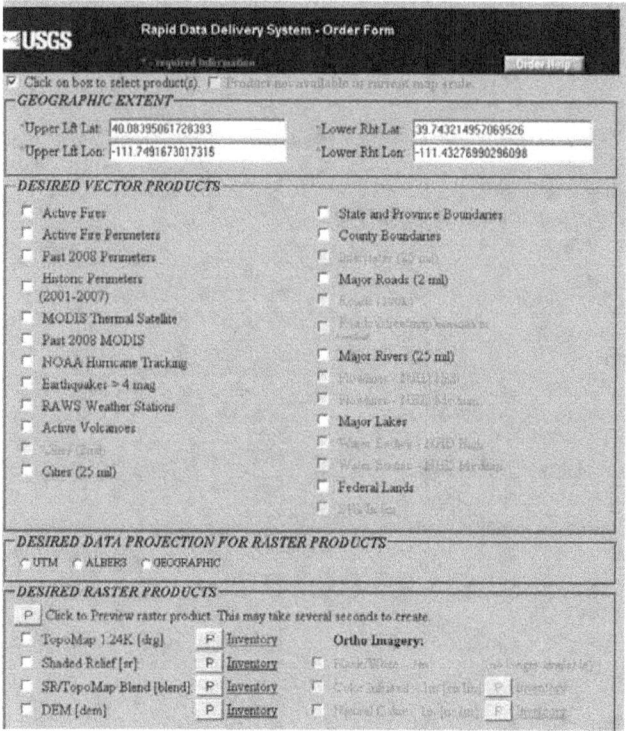

Figure 4. Products available form RDDS via the online order form.

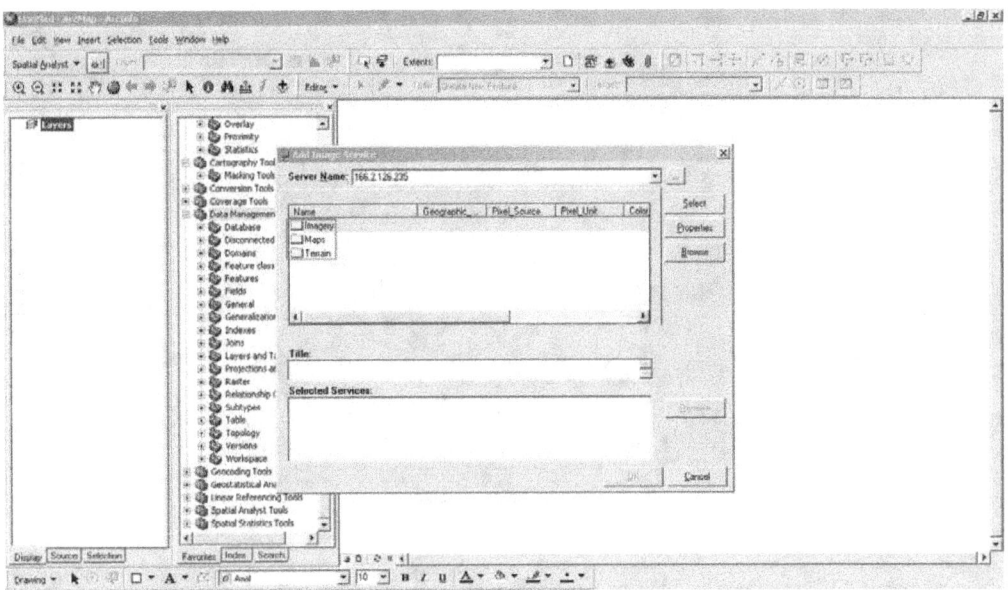

Figure 5. The USFS ArcGIS Image Server via ArcMap. The framed areas highlight the Image Server icon and the product folders available.

USFS Geodata Clearinghouse (http://fsgeodata.fs.fed.us/clearinghouse/index.html)
- This is the dissemination site for national USFS GIS data. Along with vector and raster layers, it contains maps and other data sets and resources. It is a good resource when local Forest Service information is not available; however, some data (e.g., roads, rivers) may be at a coarser resolution than desired.

National Park Service (NPS) Data Store (http://www.nps.gov/gis/data_info)
- This is the clearinghouse for NPS GIS data. The site is straight-forward – you obtain information by selecting the Park and the data type. Data on this site is uploaded and maintained by individual Parks, so the amount of information and currency will vary.

NPS — USGS National Burn Severity Mapping Project (http://burnseverity.cr.usgs.gov)
- This is a website for obtaining burn severity data for Park units from 1998 to the present. Click on **Data Archive > List View of Data – All Available Fires** to see a list of all burn severity layers available by management unit, fire name, and date.

RSAC – USGS Monitoring Trends in Burn Severity (MTBS) Website (http://svinetfc6.fs.fed. us/mtbs)
- MTBS is a multi-year project tasked to map the burn severity and perimeters of fires across the United States from 1984 to 2010. Users can download fires individually (query by year), collectively (select a year then define a box), and regionally (by year). This information can be useful to identify past fires and modify fuel and canopy characteristic layers. You can also download vector burn scar boundaries and pre- and post-fire raster scenes (fig. 6).

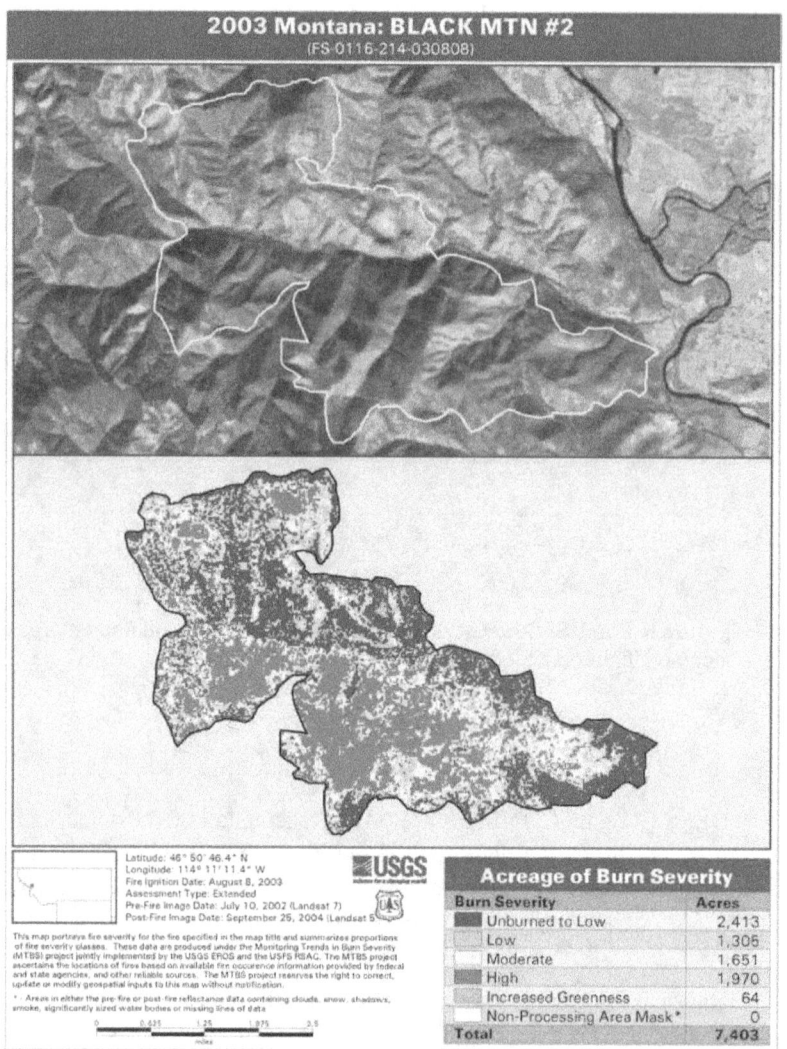

Figure 6. PDF file downloaded from MTBS for the 2003 Black Mountain 2 Fire, Missoula, MT.

Landscape Data Critque

Tabular and Graphical Critique – LCP Critique

LCP Critique is an output from FlamMap 5.0 that allows users to import an LCP and generate summary information that can be used to critique the data. The critique is in either portable document format (PDF) or text (txt) format. The text file displays the results in table form and reports individual values by class (Appendix B). The PDF displays this information as histograms and includes an image of each layer (Appendix C). Similarly, histograms can be created using ArcMap (import the layer, right click on the layer name, **Open Attribute Table** > **Options** > **Create Graph**).

Download FlamMap 5.0 (www.firemodels.org). Import an LCP. The critique can be run on the entire landscape or an analysis area. Create the txt critique by clicking on the green txt icon. Select the file location, name the critique, and click **Save**. The critique will be displayed in WordPad. Create the PDF critique by clicking on the green PDF icon. Select the file location, name the critique, and click **Save**. The PDF critique will be displayed in Acrobat.

Below is a list of items and questions to guide your critique when using the PDF and txt file output from LCP Critique. Familiarize yourself with both documents and notice how they differ. For the most part, you will spend the majority of your time using the PDF version, but refer back to the text version periodically when you need a specific value(s). Consider printing both critiques. When you find an inaccuracy or have a question, write it down in the margin for further inquiry.

(1) Check the latitude (degrees) and ensure the value is approximately in the center of your LCP. The models use latitude along with date, time, canopy cover, cloud cover, slope, and aspect to calculate solar radiation and fuel moisture.

(2) Check the cell resolution, it should be 30 m.

(3) Familiarize yourself with the units of each theme. Verify they are the same as shown in table 1.

(4) Carefully look at the *range of values* for each theme and answer the following questions:

- Is the maximum elevation consistent with the highest peak in the area?
- Does the slope exceed 90 degrees? Sometimes we think of slope in terms of degrees, but state it as percent (table 3).

Table 3. Slope conversion from degrees to percent.

Slope (degrees)	Slope (%)
5	8.7
10	17.6
15	26.8
20	36.4
25	46.6
30	57.7
35	70
40	83.9
45	100
60	173.2
80	567.128
90	inf.

- Is the range of the 13 fuel models between 1 and 13?
- Is the range of the 40 fuel models between 91 and 204?
- Does the CC exceed 70%? CC rarely exceeds 70% even in so-called closed-canopy forests (see Scott and Reinhardt 2005). Canopy cover is different than crown closure. Canopy cover refers to the horizontal proportion of the ground covered by tree crowns (e.g., bird's eye view looking down). Canopy closure, an ecological measure, is the proportion of the sky hemisphere obscured by vegetation when viewed from *a single point* (fig. 7; Jennings and others 1999). If excessive CC values exist within the modeling domain, rate of spread may be reduced due to increases in fuel moisture and the sheltering effect of the tree overstory from wind.
- Is the range of SH consistent with your knowledge of the area? Remember the values are in meters and multiplied by 10 (multiply by .3281 to calculate feet) when viewed in LCP Critique, in a text editor (e.g., WordPad), or as an individual GIS layer. The stereo photo series for quantifying natural fuels (Ottmar and others 2003) is a useful resource for canopy fuel information (http://www.fs.fed.us/pnw/fera/publications/photo_series_pubs.shtml).

USDA Forest Service Gen. Tech. Rep. RMRS-GTR-220. 2009

9

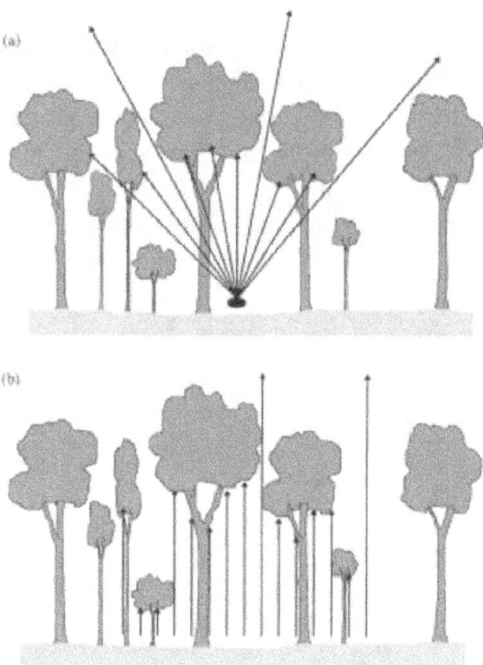

Figure 7. An example of a measure of canopy closure (a) and canopy cover (b) (Jennings and others 1999).

- Is the range of CBH consistent with your knowledge of the area? Remember the values are in meters and multiplied by 10 (multiply by .3281 to calculate feet) when viewed in LCP Critique, in a text editor, or as an individual GIS layer. *Give particular attention to CBH.* If values are too high, particularly when coupled with a modest fuel model (e.g., fuel model 8, TL3 [183]), crown fire will seldom initiate.
- Is the range of CBD consistent with your knowledge of the area? Remember the values are in kilograms per cubic meter and multiplied by 100 (divide by 100 to obtain kg/m^3) when viewed in LCP Critique, in a text editor, or as an individual GIS layer. This value is *canopy* bulk density, not crown bulk density – the entire volume of a stand vs. the volume immediately around the tree canopy (fig. 8) (Cruz and others

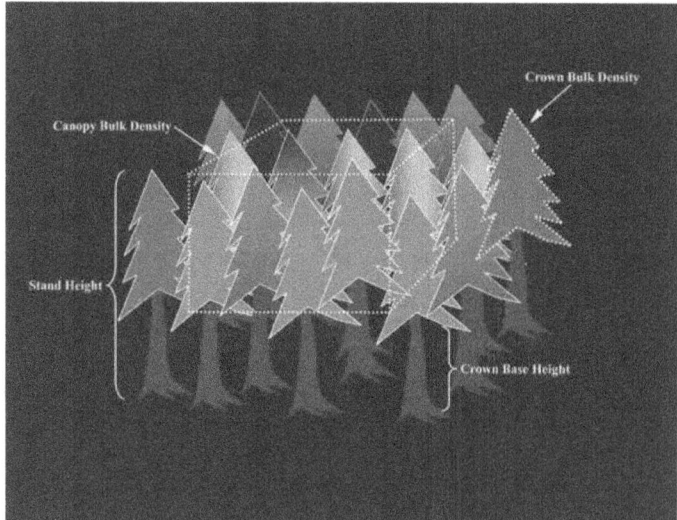

Figure 8. Stand height, crown base height, and the difference between canopy bulk density and crown bulk density (courtesy of Mark Finney).

2003). Field measurements of dense canopies (mixed conifer) have been measured at 0.25 kg m^{-3} (Scott and Reinhardt 2005), but to yield realistic crown fire estimates in FARSITE, FlamMap, and FSPro (Finney, in prep.) these upper values are often increased to 0.4+ if the default crown fire calculation method (Finney 1998) is used. If CBD values are generated from the Forest Vegetation Simulator (FVS)/Fire and Fuels Extension (FFE) (Reinhardt and Crookston 2003), FMA Plus (Carlton 2005), or FuelCalc, the program used to create LANDFIRE National data in combination with Forest Inventory and Analysis (FIA) plot information (Reinhardt and others 2006), the Scott and Reinhardt (2001) crown fire calculation method usually yields better results without manipulating the data. However, LANDFIRE Rapid Refresh data applied "canopy coefficients for adjusting CBH and CBD" to create layers suited for the Finney (1998) crown fire calculation method.

(5) Maps of each of the themes are contained in the critique and are provided for a quick visual evaluation. Look at each layer to see if the values are distributed appropriately across the landscape. Note any concerns in the margin. Later in the geospatial critique, you will be able to zoom in and query specific locations.

(6) Review the histograms (Theme Value Distributions). Start with the individual theme histograms on page one. Does the distribution look reasonable? Compare the class proportions relative to one another. What fuel models are most frequent on the landscape? Is this consistent with what you have observed? Are there any fuel models not represented that should be? If your area contains mostly grasses and shrubs, you should have a high proportion of zero values for CC, SH, CBH, and CBD. Also, study the histograms specific to each fuel model and ask the following questions: What is the proportion of rock and water to the other fuel models and to each other? Do the fuel model distributions make sense at a given elevation, slope, or aspect?

Fuel Model Comparison – Compare-Models-Four

Compare-Models-Four is an Excel application that graphically compares fire behavior output (i.e., flame length, rate of spread, fireline intensity, heat per unit area) of different fuel models given slope and fuel moisture (fig. 9). This tool can be used to familiarize yourself

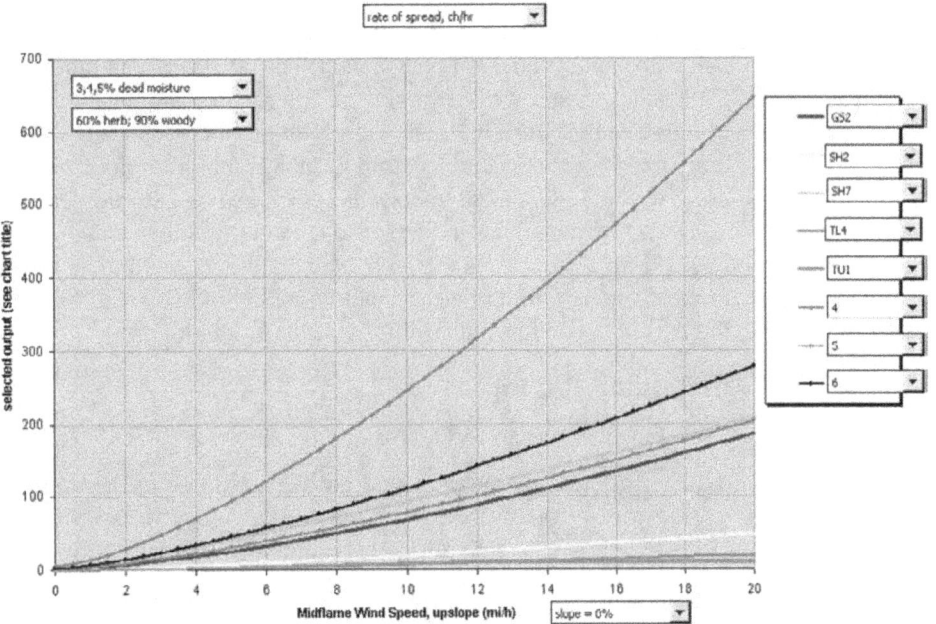

Figure 9. Rate of spread output from Compare-Models-Four for eight fuel models.

with fire behavior output generated by the new 40 fuel models compared to the 13, and to assist you in finding the "best" model for your situation. This is particularly helpful to visualize the effect that live herbaceous moisture content has on fire behavior. Compare-Models-Four can be downloaded at the FRAMES website (http://frames.nbii.gov).

Geospatial Critique – FlamMap/ArcMap

While LCP Critique is used to facilitate critiquing the LCP through tables and histograms, FlamMap can be used to spatially view and query FARSITE themes and fire modeling output. FlamMap is a geospatial fire behavior mapping and analysis program that requires an LCP, fuel moisture, and weather data. Basic FlamMap (the first two tabs) (fig. 10) makes fire

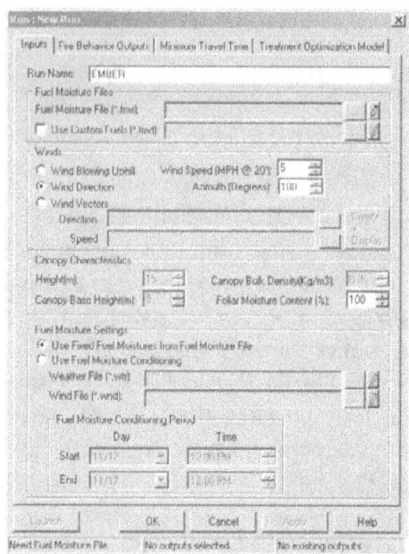

Figure 10. FlamMap new run window. Note the four tabs at the top.

behavior calculations (e.g., fireline intensity, flame length) for each location (cell) of the raster landscape, independent of one another. That is, there is no predictor of fire movement across the landscape, and weather and wind information are held constant (Finney 2006a) – think of it as a spatial Behave. Basic FlamMap output lends itself well to landscape comparisons (e.g., pre- and post-treatment) and to identifying hazardous fuel and topographic combinations, thus aiding in assessments and prioritization (Stratton 2004).

The last two modules in FlamMap are the Minimum Travel Time (MTT) (3rd tab) (Finney 2002; Finney 2006b) and the Treatment Optimization Model (TOM) (4th tab) (Finney 2006a; Finney 2006b). Familiarize yourself with FlamMap by reading the online Help and completing the six lesson tutorial (**Help > Contents > Tutorial**).

Critiquing the Inputs

(1) Open FlamMap and load an LCP (**Theme > FARSITE Landscape File**).

(2) For better viewing, expand the view (square in the upper right corner), enlarge the landscape (+ button), view the topography (click **Relief Shading**), and move the divider on the left over to the right to reveal the tree list in its entirety (fig. 11).

(3) Add any additional GIS layers that will assist you in orienting to the landscape, such as roads, trails, recreational sites, water bodies, previous fires, and prescribed fires. This

Figure 11. Modified default FlamMap window with an LCP loaded. Note the view has been expanded, landscape enlarged, relief shading selected, and horizontal divider moved to the right to reveal the tree list in its entirety.

is done by clicking the "+" to the left of Auxiliary Themes and selecting the theme type (grid or vector). Vector data is transparent (that is, you can still see the FARSITE theme); raster data must be toggled on and off. Remember FlamMap does not project on the fly, so all layers must have an identical projection when imported or they will not display.

(4) Fuel model is the default layer. To change the visible theme, click the desired layer beneath **Themes**. The default color ramps can be modified by clicking **View > Legend** or double-clicking the theme. The Create/Modify Legend window is displayed by double-clicking the legend or clicking the theme name. In the Create/Modify legend window, a user can change value colors, modify and delete classes, and save legends. Often, the fuel model default colors are hard to differentiate. Change these colors to be more distinguishable. A common practice for vegetation and fuel model layers is to color-code lower elevation fuel (e.g., grass) in light colors and higher elevation fuel (e.g., forests) in dark colors.

(5) Import the EVT layer into FlamMap. To do this, you must first convert the EVT layer you downloaded earlier from the National Map – a grid – to an ASCII RASTER. Open ArcMap, add the EVT layer to your view (**File > Add Data**) and select the ArcToolbox (**Window > ArcToolbox**). Remember the EVT layer will only be available if you used the LFDAT tool to unzip, assemble, and reproject the layer. Select **Conversion Tools > From Raster > Raster to ASCII**. Double-click on Raster to ASCII and a window will appear. Import the EVT layer, name the output, and select *.ASC for the file type. In FlamMap, click the "+" next to Auxiliary Themes, double-click **Grid Themes**, and import the EVT ASCII file. Query the landscape by double-clicking on a pixel. Note that all LCP layer values, including any auxiliary overlays such as the EVT layer, will be displayed (fig. 12). To obtain a description of the EVT code (e.g., 2011), go back to ArcMap, highlight the EVT layer, right click, and select **Open Attribute Table** (fig. 13).

(6) Import MTBS layer(s).

(7) Zoom to an area that is familiar to you (+ magnifying glass). Switch your icon back to the white arrow and double-click on the landscape. Pan around, querying the landscape

FlamMap1.fmp Point Attributes

X: 453162 Y: 4466466

Landscape | New Run

Theme	Value	Units
Elevation	1654	Meters
Slope	5	Degrees
Aspect	337	Degrees
Fuel Model	93	Class
Canopy Cover	0	Percent
Stand Height	0	Meters
Canopy Base Height	0	Meters
Canopy Bulk Density	0.000000000	kg/m^3
EVT	81.00	Class

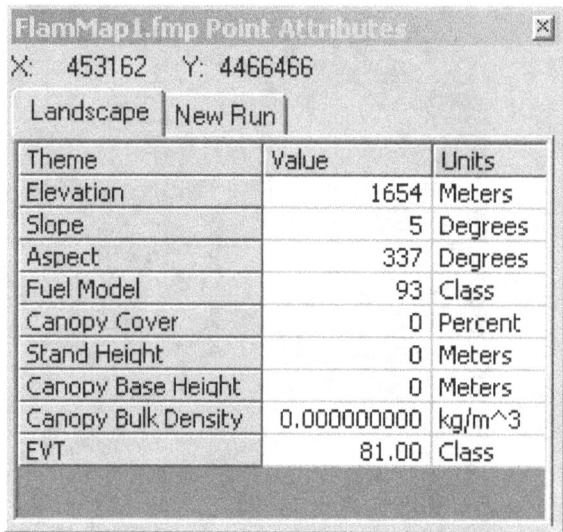

Figure 12. FlamMap point attributes dialog box that is displayed when querying the landscape. Note all the LCP layers are shown as well as the EVT layer.

Attributes of ev_type_1

Value	Count	Evt_name	Saf_srm	
11	33	Open Water	LF 11: Water	Non-vege
21	5876	Developed-Open Space	LF 20: Developed	No Domir
22	9272	Developed-Low Intensity	LF 20: Developed	No Domir
23	5428	Developed-Medium Intensity	LF 20: Developed	No Domir
24	691	Developed-High Intensity	LF 20: Developed	No Domir
31	171	Barren	LF 31: Barren	Non-vege
81	18023	Agriculture-Pasture/Hay	LF 80: Agriculture	Herbacei
82	11740	Agriculture-Cultivated Crops and Irrigated Agriculture	LF 80: Agriculture	Herbacei
2006	2	Rocky Mountain Alpine/Montane Sparsely Vegetated Systems	LF 33: Sparsely Vegetated	No Domi
2011	4432	Rocky Mountain Aspen Forest and Woodland	SAF 217: Aspen	Tree-dom
2012	41416	Rocky Mountain Bigtooth Maple Ravine Woodland	SRM 418: Bigtooth Maple	Tree-dom
2016	995	Colorado Plateau Pinyon-Juniper Woodland	SRM 504: Juniper-Pinyon Pine Woodland	Tree-dom
2019	34	Great Basin Pinyon-Juniper Woodland	SRM 412: Juniper-Pinyon Woodland	Tree-dom
2049	1	Rocky Mountain Foothill Limber Pine-Juniper Woodland	SAF 219: Limber Pine	Tree-dom
2050	3	Rocky Mountain Lodgepole Pine Forest	SAF 218: Lodgepole Pine	Tree-dom
2051	70	Southern Rocky Mountain Dry-Mesic Montane Mixed Conifer Forest and Woodland	SAF 210: Interior Douglas-Fir	Tree-dom
2052	4091	Southern Rocky Mountain Mesic Montane Mixed Conifer Forest and Woodland	SAF 211: White Fir	Tree-dom
2054	4	Southern Rocky Mountain Ponderosa Pine Woodland	SAF 237: Interior Ponderosa Pine	Tree-dom
2055	205	Rocky Mountain Subalpine Dry-Mesic Spruce-Fir Forest and Woodland	SAF 206: Engelmann Spruce-Subalpine Fir	Tree-dom
2061	1234	Inter-Mountain Basins Aspen-Mixed Conifer Forest and Woodland	SAF 217: Aspen	Tree-dom
2062	036	Inter-Mountain Basins Curl-leaf Mountain Mahogany Woodland and Shrubland	SRM 415: Curlleaf Mountain-Mahogany	Tree-dom
2070	2422	Great Basin Xeric Mixed Sagebrush Shrubland	SRM 406: Low Sagebrush	Shrub-dc
2080	1705	Inter-Mountain Basins Big Sagebrush Shrubland	SRM 403: Wyoming Big Sagebrush	Shrub-dc
2081	4	Inter-Mountain Basins Mixed Salt Desert Scrub	SRM 414: Salt Desert Shrub	Shrub-dc
2082	5	Mojave Mid-Elevation Mixed Desert Scrub	SRM 212: Blackbush	Shrub-dc
2086	718	Rocky Mountain Lower Montane-Foothill Shrubland	SRM 421: Chokecherry-Serviceberry-Rose	Shrub-dc
2103	5	Great Basin Semi Desert Chaparral	SRM 503: Arizona Chaparral	Shrub dc
2107	4402	Rocky Mountain Gambel Oak Mixed Montane Shrubland	SRM 413: Gambel oak	Shrub dc
2108	80	Sonora Mojave Semi Desert Chaparral	SRM 503: Arizona Chaparral	Shrub dc
2123	88	Columbia Plateau Steppe and Grassland	SRM 106: Bluegrass Scabland	Shrub dc
2125	228	Inter Mountain Basins Big Sagebrush Steppe	SRM 314: Big Sagebrush Bluebunch Wheatgrass	Shrub dc
2126	855	Inter Mountain Basins Montane Sagebrush Steppe	SRM 402: Mountain Big Sagebrush	Shrub dc
2127	473	Inter-Mountain Basins Semi-Desert Shrub-Steppe	SRM 403: Wyoming Big Sagebrush	Shrub-dc
2135	489	Inter-Mountain Basins Semi-Desert Grassland	SRM 502: Grama-Galetta	Herbacei
2145	1345	Rocky Mountain Subalpine-Montane Mesic Meadow	SRM 409: Tall Forb	Herbacei
2146	80	Southern Rocky Mountain Montane-Subalpine Grassland	SRM 410: Alpine Rangeland	Herbacei
2153	46	Inter-Mountain Basins Greasewood Flat	SRM 501: Saltbush-Greasewood	Shrub-dc
2154	30	Inter-Mountain Basins Montane Riparian Systems	SAF 235: Cottonwood-Willow	Tree-dom

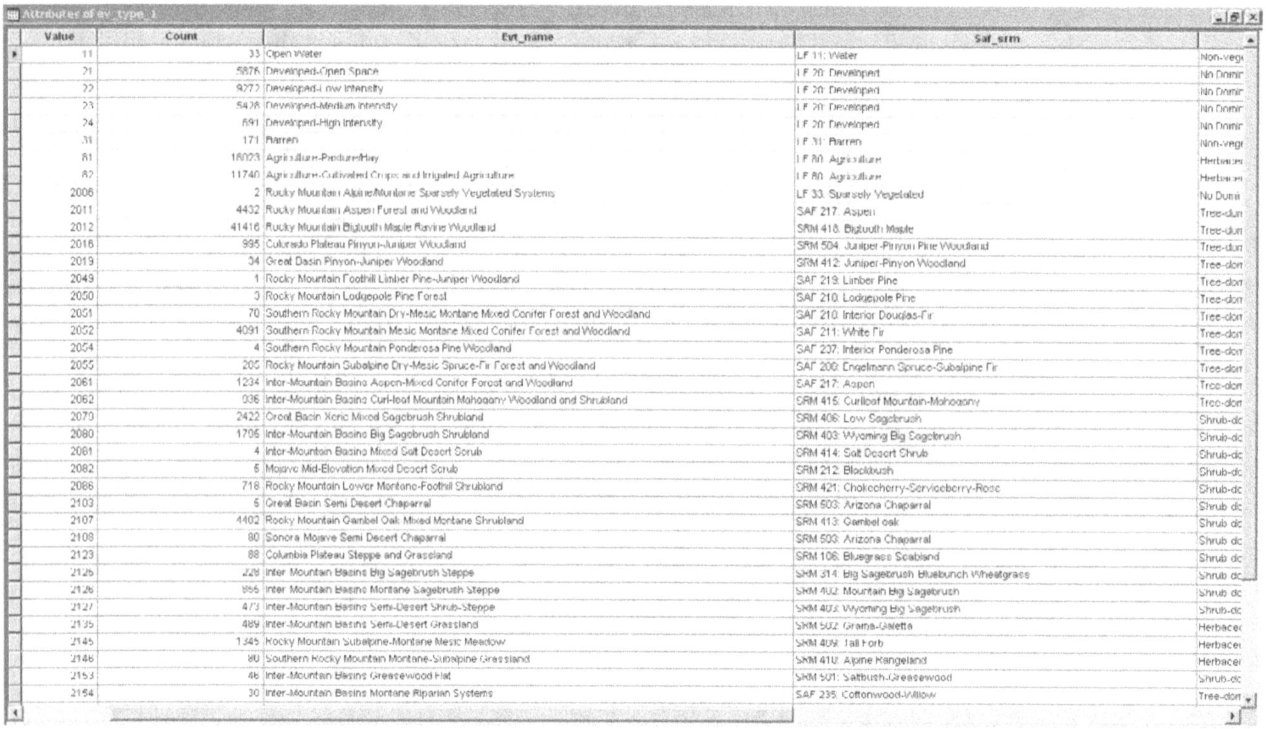

Figure 13. Sample EVT layer attributes from ArcMap.

frequently. Do these values make sense? Zoom to another area familiar to you (e.g., a recent fire or prescribed burn site). Are recent disturbances accounted for? If so, are the fuel models and canopy assignments adequate? A good practice is to view lakes, large rivers, and barren areas and assess if the LANDFIRE layers captured the non-burnable areas and assigned them a suitable fuel model (98 or 99). It is also a good idea to look at agricultural lands and high elevation meadows. Sometimes these areas are mapped incorrectly. Refer back to the PDF summary fuel model histogram. Where are those highest frequency fuel models located on the landscape? Continue to sample the landscape in this manner evaluating all of the fuel models represented. Note any concerns or changes that need to be made on the margin of the appropriate PDF LCP Critique map output.

(8) An alternative method to associating the EVT layer with the FARSITE layers is done in ArcMap or ArcView. For the sake of consistency, the ArcMap approach is outlined. However, this same procedure can be done in ArcView using the Grid Analyst Extension.

Open ArcMap and add the EVT grid layer, as well as the fuel and canopy layers used to create the FARSITE LCP (Fuel Model, CC, SH, CBH, CBD). In this example, the following is a simple procedure to combine the 40 fuel models with CC and EVT. Select **View > Tool-Bars > Spatial Analyst**. Select **Spatial Analyst > Raster Calculator**. In the input window, type the name of the new grid to be created (e.g., Combo), an equal sign, and the command "combine." After the combine command, select each grid to be combined by double-clicking the grid in the upper window. Once the expression is complete (fig. 14), click **Evaluate**. The Raster Calculator creates a new grid that combines the individual grids. Select the new grid (highlight it), right click, and select **Open Attribute Table**. Click on **Count** – the column will be displayed in blue – then right click on **Count**, and select **Sort Descending**.

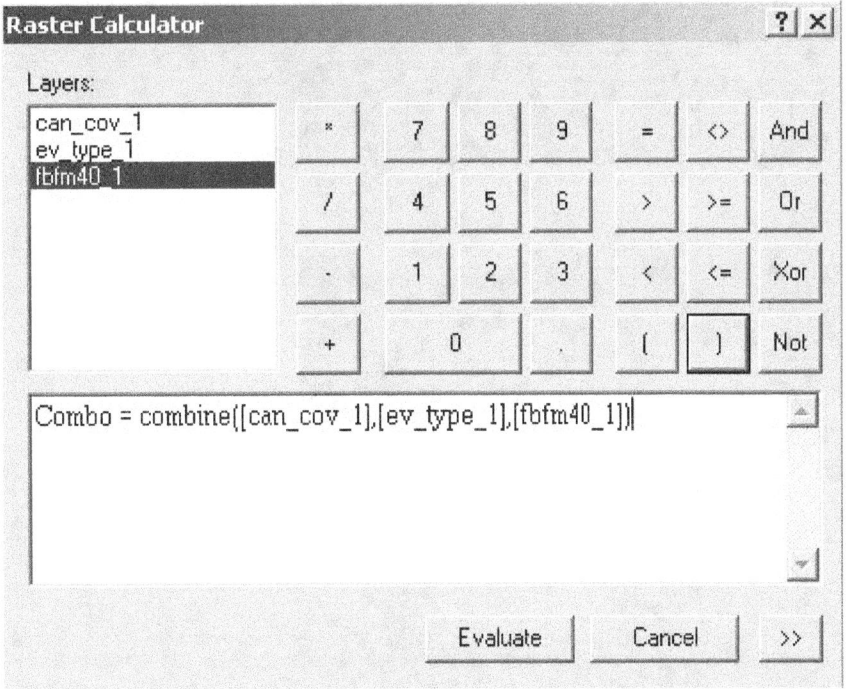

Figure 14. The expression used in the ArcMap Raster Calculator to combine the EVT layer with the 40 fuel models and canopy cover.

Figure 15 is an attribute table of a combined grid of the 40 fuel models, canopy cover, and EVT. Any combination of grids can be combined (e.g., CBH, CBD, and fuel model). Note the column count (the number of cell values) is sorted in descending order. Look at the 4th row down. There are 6,661 30 x 30 m cells that are a fuel model 146 (low load, humid climate shrub) and have a canopy cover of zero and an EVT of 2017 (Gambel oak).

To see the spatial distribution of the 6,661 cells, select the entire row by clicking on the small gray square to the left of the ObjectID column (framed in red in fig. 15). Add other GIS layers to the view such as roads, streams, historical fires, and topography to provide spatial context (fig. 16) and ask the following questions: Are the locations of the higher frequency grid combinations correct? Does the EVT classification "match" with the fuel model assignment? Are the canopy characteristics adequate given the EVT, fuel model, and spatial location? Overlay recent disturbances, are they accounted for? Is the mapping of the fuel models and canopy characteristics adequate? Google Earth is an excellent tool to view imagery of a specific area and compare it to LANDFIRE fuel layers, particularly in areas of disturbance.

Figure 15. Attribute table of a combined grid of EVT, fuel model, and canopy cover. The count column (highlighted in blue) has been sorted in descending order. Clicking the gray square (in red) to the left of the ObjectID will select all the values in the row with a count of 6,661.

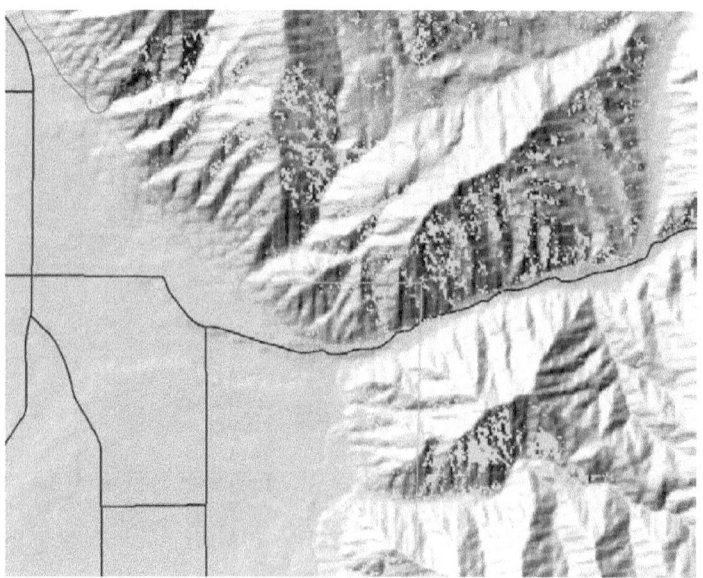

Figure 16. Areas of fuel model 146, with no CC and an EVT of 2217 (Gambel oak) draped on a shaded relief and overlaid with a fire perimeter (red), roads (black), and the forest boundary (green).

Examining the Outputs

Once you have scrutinized the LANDFIRE data both numerically and visually, you are ready to examine the data and models based on fire behavior output. Analyzing the outputs can validate suspicions one has when critiquing the inputs and reveal new problems.

Before we proceed with the geospatial critique, there are a few things that are important to remember about models (adapted from Stratton 2006).

- "A model is a simplification or approximation of reality and hence will not reflect all of reality" (Burnham and Anderson 1998). George Box (1979) stated, "All models are wrong, but some are useful." It is the task of the modeler to select the appropriate model, produce usable output, and interpret model findings given model assumptions and limitations. However, it is the client that ultimately determines the usefulness of the model.
- Modeling is an art as well as a science and one's field experience enables the art of the modeler. Be mindful that a model is a decision support tool, not a tool that makes decisions.
- A variety of programs and tools support wildland fire management. For example, there are systems to predict fire growth and behavior, tools and information on fire effects, and smoke models for dispersion and emission estimates. Fire models, such as FARSITE and BehavePlus (Andrews and others 2005) are actually *fire modeling systems* that link multiple empirical and deterministic models or set(s) of mathematical equations to predict fire growth and behavior. Each model (e.g., surface spread model [Rothermel 1972] or spotting model [Albini 1979]) has assumptions and limitations, and can be applied differently in the modeling systems. It is important that users understand model limitations and assumptions and know how these models are used in the fire modeling systems.
- Remember models are "...artful applications of existing knowledge. They do not attempt to explain the physics or mechanics...As the science of surface and crown fire behavior advances, so too will our fire management applications" (Scott 2006).
- Most fire management programs have online Help and tutorials. Consult these resources first before asking for assistance from subject matter experts (SMEs).

(1) Work with local SMEs to identify three historical fires that represent different weather and fuel moisture scenarios (e.g., moderate, high, and extreme). Gather perimeter, fuel moisture, wind, and weather information. Your goal is to know enough about the fire environment prior and during the event to simulate this environment as you critique the data in FlamMap and possibly calibrate the model in FARSITE or FlamMap. Choose a scenario and proceed to step 2.

(2) Load the LCP into FlamMap. From the tree pane select **Analysis Areas > Runs**. Double-click **Runs** and the new run window will be displayed.

(3) Name your run. Create a fuel moisture file (.fms) that corresponds to the chosen historical fire scenario. If fuel moisture information is available (e.g., from fire records or a nearby sampling site), create and/or modify the .fms file using FARSITE **(Input > Project Inputs)**. A useful site for live and dead sampling information is the National Fuel Moisture Database (http://72.32.186.224/nfmd/public/index.php). Calculated values for fuel moisture can be obtained from FireFamily Plus (Bradshaw and McCormick 2000) using the Daily Listing (**Weather > Seasonal Reports > Daily Listing**), if a weather and wind file has been obtained (see step six). Figure 17 contains fuel moisture file scenarios from BehavePlus (**Configure > Moisture scenario set selection**) for a given fuel moisture condition (e.g., very low dead, fully cured herb, or D1L1 [D=dead/L=live/1 denotes the first scenario]).

(4) Import the wind speed and direction. You can specify wind blowing uphill (worst-case), a specific speed and direction, or an ASCII Raster wind vector (e.g., wind speed and direction grid derived from WindWizard) (fig. 18; Butler and others 2004, 2006). For the purposes of the critique, select **Wind Blowing Uphill** and input a wind speed suitable to the scenario you are modeling.

FuelModeling	16	Used to develop new fuel models (Scott and Burgan)
d1l1.bpm		D1L1 - Very low dead, fully cured herb (3,4,5,30,60)
d1l2.bpm		D1L2 - Very low dead, 2/3 cured herb (3,4,5,60,90)
d1l3.bpm		D1L3 - Very low dead, 1/3 cured herb (3,4,5,90,120)
d1l4.bpm		D1L4 - Very low dead, fully green herb (3,4,5,120,150)
d2l1.bpm		D2L1 - Low dead, fully cured herb (6,7,8,30,60)
d2l2.bpm		D2L2 - Low dead, 2/3 cured herb (6,7,8,60,90)
d2l3.bpm		D2L3 - Low dead, 1/3 cured herb (6,7,8,90,120)
d2l4.bpm		D2L4 - Low dead, fully green herb (6,7,8,120,150)
d3l1.bpm		D3L1 - Moderate dead, fully cured herb (9,10,11,30,60)
d3l2.bpm		D3L2 - Moderate dead, 2/3 cured herb (9,10,11,60,90)
d3l3.bpm		D3L3 - Moderate dead, 1/3 cured herb (9,10,11,90,120)
d3l4.bpm		D3L4 - Moderate dead, fully green herb (9,10,11,120,150)
d4l1.bpm		D4L1 - High dead, fully cured herb (12,13,14,30,60)
d4l2.bpm		D4L2 - High dead, 2/3 cured herb (12,13,14,60,90)
d4l3.bpm		D4L3 - High dead, 1/3 cured herb (12,13,14,90,120)
d4l4.bpm		D4L4 - High dead, fully green herb (12,13,14,120,150)

Figure 17. Fuel moisture file scenarios from BehavePlus.

Figure 18. Gridded Wind (100 m) derived from a fluid dynamics model based on 25+ mph ridgetop winds from the southwest in the Goat Mountain area (Boise National Forest, ID). Wind vectors are colored by speed with 0 to 4 mph (blue), 5 to 7 (green), 8 to 11 (yellow), 12 to 15 (orange), and 16+ (red).

(5) The default foliar moisture content (FMC) is an adequate starting point. Foliar moisture affects crown fire initiation and occurrence. FMC generally ranges from 75 to 150 (see Scott and Reinhardt 2001). Lowering the FMC – a landscape-wide adjustment – will increase torching and crowning. This can be a quick technique to ascertain the "nearness" the landscape is to crown fire initiation without manipulating the canopy themes.

(6) Obtain FARSITE weather (.wtr) and wind (.wnd) files for your modeling scenario to condition the fuels. Conditioning fuels is important or all fuel models irrespective of topography, cover, or weather will start at the *values specified in the .fms file* (fig. 19). Condition about 1 week prior to the event and have the simulation start time correspond with the fuel moisture values.

Figure 19. FlamMap 1-hour fuel moisture (1 to 10%) output for the Wasatch Front, UT (looking east). Fuels have been conditioned based on elevation, cover, and weather at 1400 hours.

If weather and wind files are not available, locate the nearest RAWS, download the data from either the Kansas City Fire Access Software (KCFAST) (USFS 1996) site (http://famtest.nwcg.gov/fam-web/kcfast/html/wxmenu.htm) or the Western Regional Climate Center (WRCC) (http://www.wrcc.dri.edu/wraws), and import them into FireFamily Plus. A detailed description of this process is contained in Stratton (2006; p. 5-7). You can also construct weather and wind files in FARSITE (**Input > Project Inputs**), but the process can be time consuming and you still need station weather and wind information to create the files.

(7) Select **Fire Behavior Outputs** (tab 2). Select **Fireline Intensity**, **Rate of Spread**, **Flame Length**, and **Crown Fire Activity**. Note that the default crown fire calculation method is set to Finney 1998.

(8) Click **Apply** and **Launch**. FlamMap conditioning and calculations should be completed in a couple minutes. Click **OK** and close the run window.

(9) Click on the + to the left of your new run. The four fire behavior outputs will be listed. Complete two more runs (**Analysis Area > New Run**) representing the other two scenarios. Critique the outputs as guided below.

Flame Length

Flame length (FL or L) is defined as the distance from the midpoint of the active flaming front to the average tip of the flames (Andrews 2008) (fig. 20). Flame length is calculated from fireline intensity. FARSITE/FlamMap uses Byram's (1959) equation to predict FL ($L = 0.45I^{0.46}$ ft; I is fireline intensity). Thomas' (1963) equation ($L = 0.2I^{2/3}$ ft) is used to predict flame length for passive and active crown fire (Finney 1998).

View the FL output. Look at the default legend and note the range of values. For viewing simplification, view flame length using the predefined hauling chart legend (**Create/Modify Legend > Predefined Legend > Hauling Categories**) (fig. 21).

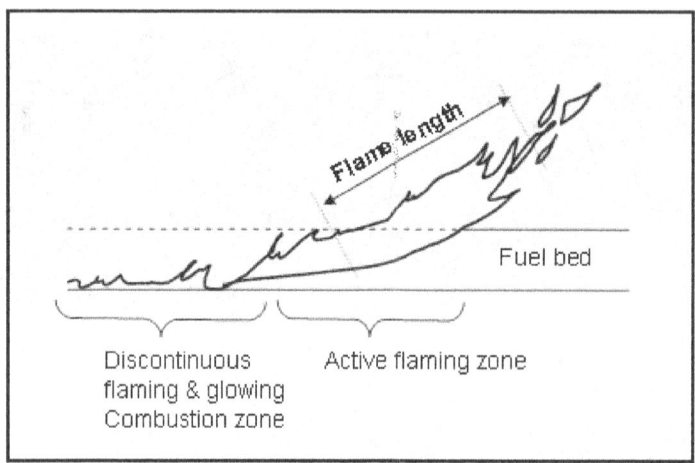

Figure 20. Depiction of flame length as measured from the midpoint of the active flaming zone to the average tip of the flames (from Andrews 1986).

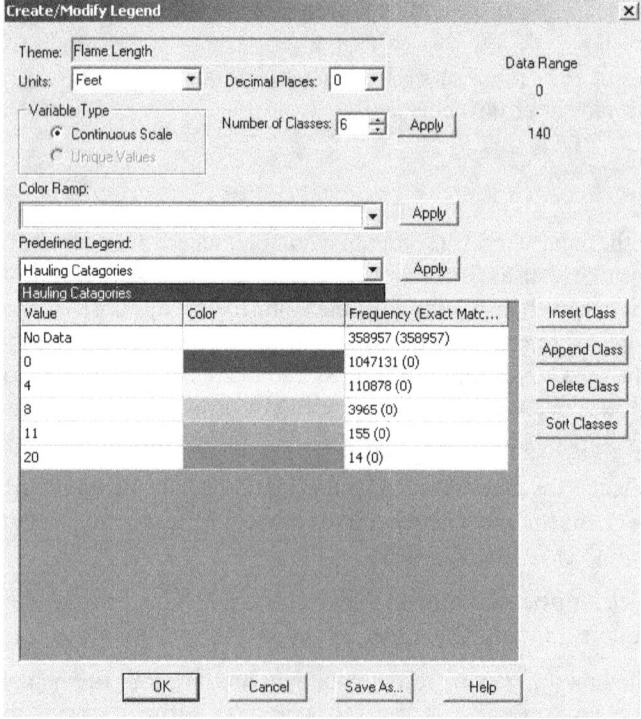

Figure 21. FlamMap Create/Modify Legend window. Note the predefined legend of the hauling categories for flame length.

Model calculations of flame lengths for shallow surface fuels are generally adequate. However, model estimates of flame length in crown fires or deep fuel beds sometimes appear less than field observations. This discrepancy is usually a result of (1) an inaccurate ocular estimate or perception of flame length or (2) the model is in fact underestimating flame length because of an underprediction in fireline intensity.

(1) Remember, when estimating flame length, particularly in aerial fuels, flames often originate well above the surface, yet we view these flames *relative to the ground*. So make sure you are measuring them correctly and keep in mind, "flame length is an elusive parameter that exists in the eye of the beholder. It is a poor quantity to use in a scientific or engineering sense, but it is so readily apparent to fireline personnel and so readily conveys a sense of fire intensity that it is worth featuring as a primary fire variable" (Rothermel 1991).

(2) An underestimate of flame length in canopy fuels often occurs when using the Finney (1998) crown fire calculation method. This is due to a lack of crown fire that results in a lower fireline intensity. If higher flame lengths are expected, use the Scott and Reinhardt (2001) crown fire calculation method.

Flame length output is best critiqued as a relative trend evaluation from low to high. Zoom to a familiar area where flame length should be low or zero (e.g., a recent burn or a body of water). Are the values what you would expect? Move to areas that you would expect moderate and high flame lengths. Are these values adequate? Sometimes fire behavior outputs are better understood when viewed in relation to a familiar fuel model (e.g., fuel model 8 or 10), so query a particular cell and use Compare-Models-Four to compare the query with the standard.

Rate of Spread

Like FL, critique rate of spread (ROS) in a relative sense, from low to high. Change the default legend to a predefined legend (**Create/Modify Legend > Predefined Legend > Chains per Hour**). Zoom to a familiar area where ROS should be low or zero. Are the values what you would expect? Move to areas of moderate and high ROS. Are the values consistent with your fire behavior knowledge? Again, compare the output values to other fuel models using the comparison tool.

Fireline Intensity

Fireline intensity (FLI or I) is the product of the rate of spread and heat generated from the available fuel during flaming combustion [$I = Rwh$, Btu/ft·sec; where R is rate of spread, ft/s, w is available fuel, lb/ft², and h is heat of combustion, Btu/lb] (Byram 1959). Reduce the number of classes to six (includes a no data category) and the decimal places to zero. Change the default color ramp to the *last* ramp (blue-green-yellow-orange-red) (**Create/Modify Legend > Color Ramp**) (fig. 22). Change the classes to 58, 100, 500, 1,000, and the maximum value (see the range of values in the upper right of the Create/Modify Legend window) (see fig. 22).

Zoom to a familiar area where FLI should be low or zero (that is, an area you could extinguish with hand tools). Using tables 4 and 5, are the values what you would expect? Move to areas of moderate and high FLI and ask the same question. An upper limit for large wildland fires is 30,000 Btu/ft·sec. The Sundance Fire (1967) in northern Idaho, which traveled 16 miles in 9 hours with crowning, long-range spotting, and tree breakage and blowdown, had an estimated intensity of 22,500 Btu/ft·sec (Anderson 1968).

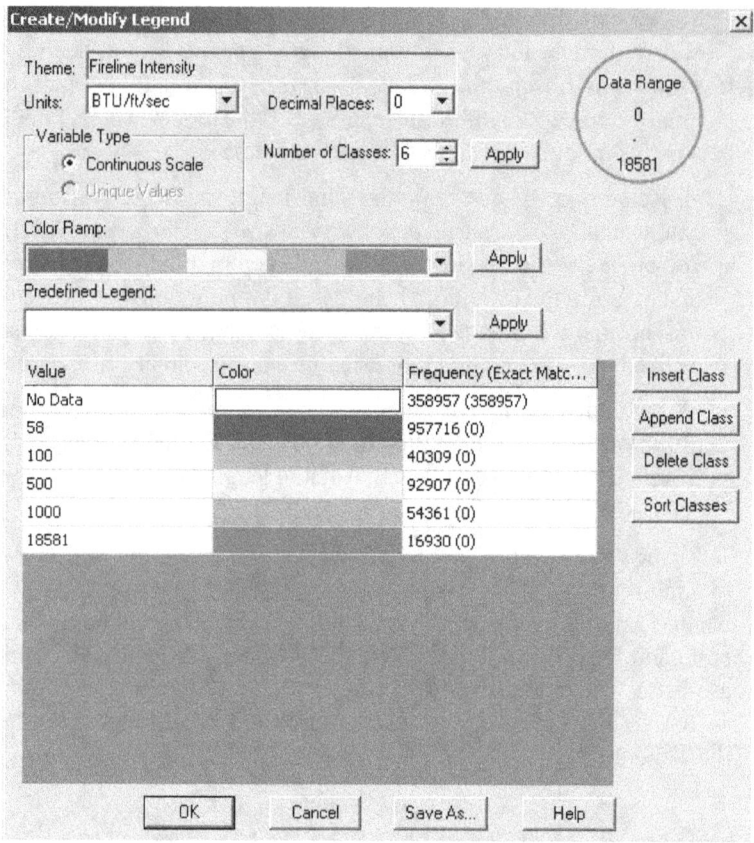

Figure 22. FlamMap Create/Modify Legend window. Fireline intensity has been grouped into five classes, plus no data, zero decimal places specified, and a blue to red color ramp. The data range is noted in the upper right (red circle).

Table 4. Fire description and suppression interpretations of flame length and fireline intensity (principally adapted from Andrews and Rothermel 1982).

Flame length	Fireline intensity	Fire description and suppression interpretations
(ft)	*(BTU/Ft·Sec)*	
~2	19 - 58	Most prescribed fires burning against the wind. Depth of the flaming zone (front to back) would be less than 1 ft and the flame length about 2 ft. Could easily step over the fire without fear of injury (Byram 1959; Roussopoulos and Johnson 1975).
<4	<100	Fire can generally be attacked at the head or flanks by persons using handtools. Handline should hold the line.
4 - 8	100 - 500	Fires are too intense for direct attack on the head by persons using handtools. Handline cannot be relied on to hold fire. Equipment such as plows, dozers, pumpers, and retardant aircraft, can be effective.
8 - 11	500 - 1,000	Fires may present serious control problems—torching out, crowning, and spotting. Control efforts at the fire head will probably be ineffective.
>11	>1,000	Crowning, spotting, and major fire runs are probable. Control efforts at head of fire are ineffective.

Table 5. Fireline intensity equivalents to flame lengths as calculated by Thomas' (1963) model (in Rothermel 1991).

Flame length	Fireline intensity
(ft)	*(Btu/ft·sec)*
20	1,000
30	1,840
40	2,830
50	3,950
75	7,260
100	11,200
125	15,600
150	20,500
175	25,900
200	31,600
225	37,700
250	44,200
275	51,000
300	58,100

Crown Fire Activity

Crown fire activity (CFA) is probably the most important fire behavior output you will critique. This single output gives you an indication if the combination of fuel model, SH, CBH, and CBD is adequately mapped to generate the fire behavior you expect. Crown fire initiation is dependent on several factors, including surface FLI, canopy foliar moisture, and CBH (VanWagner 1977). CBH is used to determine if torching occurs. CBD affects transition to an active crown fire.

The CFA theme was derived using the default crown fire calculation method (Finney 1998). Do another run using the Scott and Reinhardt (2001) calculation method (Fire Behavior Outputs tab). Given identical environmental inputs, it is common to see a difference in CFA between the two crown fire calculation methods (fig. 23). This is due to a difference in the crown fraction burned transition function. When using *LANDFIRE National data*, the Scott and Reinhardt (2001) method frequently yields a more realistic CFA map.

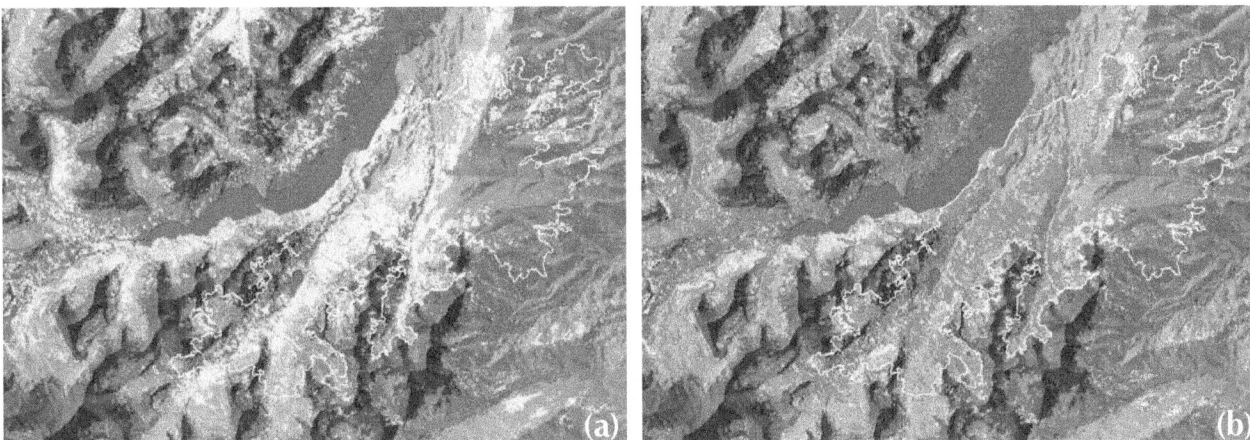

Figure 23. Crown fire activity output from FlamMap using the Finney (1998) (a) and Scott and Reinhardt (2001) (b) crown fire calculation methods. Gray areas are rock and water, pea green is surface fire, yellow is passive crown fire (torching), and red is active crown fire. The white perimeter (32,000 acres) is the Red Eagle Fire (August 2006) in Glacier National Park, MT. The fire consisted of several high intensity crown fire runs to the NE (upper right corner).

Compare both CFA themes. In general, which is most consistent with observed fire behavior? Are there areas of surface fire that you suspect would burn as a crown fire or visa-versa? Why might that be? Overlay the MTBS layer and compare areas of high severity with crown fire occurrence. Keep in mind, areas of high severity do not always equate to high intensity, but based on your knowledge of fire behavior in that fuel complex, you can determine if the correlation is appropriate.

Wind speed and foliar moisture content affect CFA. Try modifying the wind speed or lowering the foliar moisture content – landscape wide adjustments – and see how that affects model output. These simple adjustments will give you a quick indication of how "close" your fuel layers are to torching and crowning. A general rule of thumb is flame length needs to be greater than ½ the CBH for crown fire initiation (table 6). Note if the FMC is 100% and the CBH is 5 m, the flame length needed to transition to a crown fire is 2.5 m.

Table 6. Table of flame length (L_o) (m) for a given foliar moisture content (FMC) (% oven dried weight basis) and live crown base height (LCBH) (m) based on Byram (1959) and Van Wagner (1977) (in Alexander 1988).

LCBH (m)	FMC (% ODW basis) L_o (m)											
	75	80	85	90	95	100	105	110	115	120	125	130
0.5	0.4	0.4	0.5	0.5	0.5	0.5	0.5	0.5	0.6	0.6	0.6	0.6
1.0	0.7	0.7	0.7	0.8	0.8	0.8	0.8	0.9	0.9	0.9	0.9	1.0
1.5	0.9	1.0	1.0	1.0	1.1	1.1	1.1	1.1	1.2	1.2	1.2	1.3
2.0	1.1	1.2	1.2	1.2	1.3	1.3	1.4	1.4	1.4	1.5	1.5	1.5
2.5	1.3	1.4	1.4	1.5	1.5	1.5	1.6	1.6	1.7	1.7	1.8	1.8
3.0	1.5	1.5	1.6	1.6	1.7	1.8	1.8	1.9	1.9	2.0	2.0	2.0
3.5	1.7	1.7	1.8	1.8	1.9	1.9	2.0	2.1	2.1	2.2	2.2	2.3
4.0	1.8	1.9	1.9	2.0	2.1	2.1	2.2	2.3	2.3	2.4	2.4	2.5
4.5	2.0	2.0	2.1	2.2	2.2	2.3	2.4	2.5	2.5	2.6	2.6	2.7
5.0	2.1	2.2	2.3	2.3	2.4	2.5	2.6	2.6	2.7	2.8	2.8	2.9
5.5	2.3	2.3	2.4	2.5	2.6	2.7	2.7	2.8	2.9	3.0	3.0	3.1
6.0	2.4	2.5	2.6	2.7	2.7	2.8	2.9	3.0	3.1	3.2	3.2	3.3
6.5	2.5	2.6	2.7	2.8	2.9	3.0	3.1	3.2	3.2	3.3	3.4	3.5
7.0	2.7	2.8	2.9	3.0	3.1	3.1	3.2	3.3	3.4	3.5	3.6	3.7
7.5	2.8	2.9	3.0	3.1	3.2	3.3	3.4	3.5	3.6	3.7	3.8	3.9
8.0	2.9	3.0	3.1	3.2	3.3	3.4	3.5	3.6	3.7	3.8	3.9	4.0
8.5	3.0	3.2	3.3	3.4	3.5	3.6	3.7	3.8	3.9	4.0	4.1	4.2
9.0	3.2	3.3	3.4	3.5	3.6	3.7	3.8	4.0	4.1	4.2	4.3	4.4
9.5	3.3	3.4	3.5	3.7	3.8	3.9	4.0	4.1	4.2	4.3	4.4	4.5
10	3.4	3.5	3.7	3.8	3.9	4.0	4.1	4.3	4.4	4.5	4.6	4.7
11	3.6	3.8	3.9	4.0	4.2	4.3	4.4	4.5	4.7	4.8	4.9	5.0
12	3.9	4.0	4.2	4.3	4.4	4.6	4.7	4.8	5.0	5.1	5.2	5.3
13	4.1	4.2	4.4	4.5	4.7	4.8	5.0	5.1	5.2	5.4	5.5	5.6
14	4.3	4.5	4.6	4.8	4.9	5.1	5.2	5.4	5.5	5.7	5.8	5.9
15	4.5	4.7	4.8	5.0	5.2	5.3	5.5	5.6	5.8	5.9	6.1	6.2

Fire Growth

The next critique is to evaluate fire growth for a short duration (a one or two day spread event). To do this, we use MTT (as stated earlier, a module in FlamMap). A rectangular lattice is draped over the FARSITE LCP. FlamMap calculates 2-D spread rates and a max spread direction at each cell. Holding all environmental conditions constant, the MTT algorithm searches for the fastest path of fire spread along straight-line transects connected by nodes (cell corners) (Finney 2006b). MTT pathways are then interpolated to reveal the fire perimeter positions at an instant in time (fig. 24). These perimeters are similar to wave-front expansion (FARSITE) but are mathematically and computationally more efficient (Finney 2002).

(1) Select one of your three fire scenarios and import historical fire progression information into FlamMap as a vector file.

Figure 24. Depiction of fire spread using MTT (courtesy of Mark Finney).

(2) Draw an ignition(s) on the landscape to coincide with the start of the previous fire perimeter. Save the ignitions (**Options > Ignitions > Save to File**). In the run window, click **MTT** and load the ignition (**Load Current Ignitions**). You can also import an ignition file (e.g., the previous day's perimeter) if it is in shapefile format and *in the same projection*. This is done by selecting the MTT tab, and in the Ignitions box, clicking the **From File** load button (three dots on the right).

(3) Set the simulation time (in minutes) to match the spread event you are calibrating. The defaults for resolution and interval for minimal travel paths are usually adequate. For outputs, select flow paths, major paths, and arrival time contour. Click **Apply** and **Launch**.

(4) Click **OK** and close the run window. Displayed will be the flow paths (black), major paths (yellow), and contours (blue). The elevation grid ramped with a couple dark colors is usually a good way to view the major paths and contours (fig. 25).

(5) Compare the MTT run with the actual fire perimeter. How is the "fit" on the flank, rear, and head? If there is a major discrepancy, why might that be? Conduct additional runs to problem solve by varying the maximum simulation time, fuel moisture, wind speed and direction, spotting, etc. Were reasonable changes in environmental factors and model parameters adequate to fit the historical fire perimeter? If not, what other variables could be a factor (e.g., fuel model, CBH)? Figure 26 shows the fire perimeter of the Price Canyon Fire (a 9-hr run) compared to a FARSITE simulation. This scenario would be a good candidate to critique fire growth using MTT.

Figure 25. MTT major paths (yellow) for the Dammeron Fire (in red; 9,982 acres). Land managers were interested in knowing which section of the perimeter would first reach the valley bottom (Pine Valley, UT) if the fire advanced from its present location in the wilderness area during a high wind event.

Figure 26. FARSITE calibration exercise on the Price Canyon Fire (June 2002; Helper, UT). The white polygon is the fire perimeter at 10 p.m. (2,900 ac). A train started the fire at 2 p.m. (smallest green perimeter) and proceeded to burn into the "bowl" to the north (top left) and Sulphur Canyon to the east. The dirt road to the north was imported as a barrier. This scenario would be a good candidate to critique fire growth using MTT.

Editing and Updating the LCP

Most LCPs from LANDFIRE will require minor to moderate edits. As an analyst, you want to incorporate your critique's findings to improve model output. On the other hand, there are usually time restraints that limit how long you can take preparing the LCP. It is important to focus on the changes that affect the most ground (pixels) and not get bogged down worrying about the minutia. Keep in mind, you are doing landscape fire growth modeling with imperfect data and models.

If modifications to the LCP are warranted, there are three sources of error: data, user, and model (DUM) (see McHugh 2006). Often we are too quick to accuse the model when the data are the source of the problem. Adjust the fuel model layer first, followed by CBH and CC (Stratton 2006). It is a good idea to keep a log of changes in case further into the procedure you start seeing things that are suspicious and need to backtrack. Also, make changes incrementally. If you make several changes all at once, it is difficult to assess how a specific change affected a given fire behavior output.

There are two tools specific to editing and updating *an LCP*: the FARSITE landscape calculator and the WFDSS landscape editor. These tools are generally used to make straightforward changes to LCPs (e.g., account for recent burns, changes to fuel models). Complex changes are made using a GIS or an ArcMap extension, such as the Area Change Tool (ACT) (NIFTT 2008) or the Raster Change Tool (RCT) (Thompson, in prep.).

Making Modest Changes to the LCP

FARSITE Landscape Calculator

The WFDSS editor and the FARSITE calculator allow you to perform mathematical or logical operations on individual FARSITE themes without the use of a GIS. The FARSITE landscape calculator uses a single window to help users construct and execute expressions (fig. 27). It takes time to learn, is limited in its capabilities, and enhancements to the program are not planned. The WFDSS landscape editor is similar to the FARSITE landscape calculator, but is web-based, easier to use, and supported for the foreseeable future.

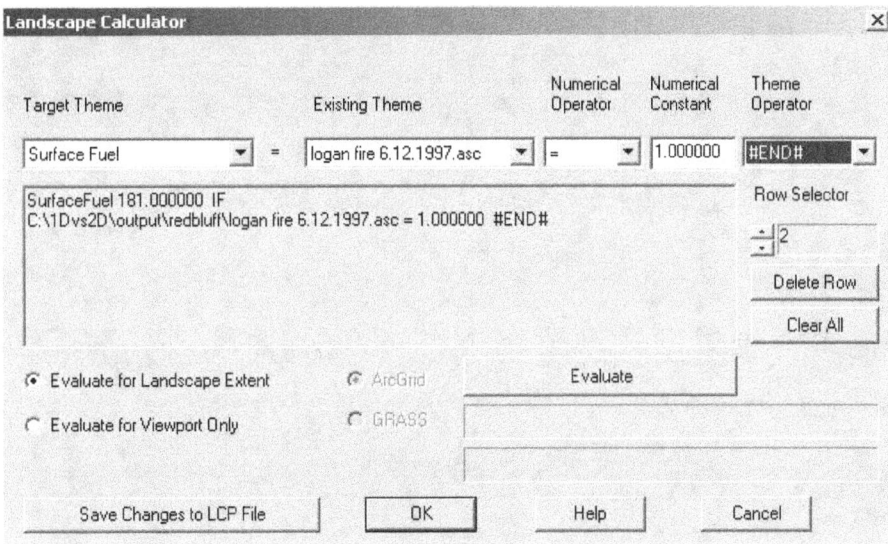

Figure 27. The FARSITE landscape calculator. Note the expression to convert the Logan fire to TL1 (181).

USDA Forest Service Gen. Tech. Rep. RMRS-GTR-220. 2009

27

WFDSS Landscape Editor

To use the landscape editor, an incident must be created by WFDSS (**Incident > New Incidents**) and/or imported (LCP must be zipped with a projection file). Once this is done, click on **View Information**, **Landscape**, and **LCP Editor**. The landscape file editor window will be displayed. Read the bulleted information and then click **Add Rule**. The add landscape editor rule window will be displayed. Read the bulleted information to the right on how to use the tool.

Below are several scenarios and the changes that were made to LANDFIRE LCPs by applying a rule set. Once all rules are imported, save the rule set, and create a new LCP.

Change in Fuel Model

Issue: Areas of fuel model SH4 (144; low load, humid climate timber-shrub) are located on dry, steep slopes.

Resolution: After carefully querying the landscape and viewing imagery in Google Earth, areas of SH4 contained sparse shrub – SH1 (141; low load dry climate shrub) (fig. 28).

Issue: Areas with steep slopes (40+ degrees) were mapped as GR1 (101) and GR2 (102), but were not carrying fire.

Resolution: After viewing these areas in Google Earth, NB9 (99; bare ground) was selected as the replacement fuel model (fig. 29).

Issue: Several recent fires are not accounted for in the LCP.

Resolution: A GIS layer of fires from 2000 to 2006 was obtained from the local unit (sc-fires_00_06). This layer was uploaded to WFDSS (**Incidents > View Information > Shape Upload**). Field intelligence indicated that fires from 2000 to 2006 were "holding." Fuel model TL1 (181; low load compact conifer litter) was selected as the replacement fuel model (fig. 30).

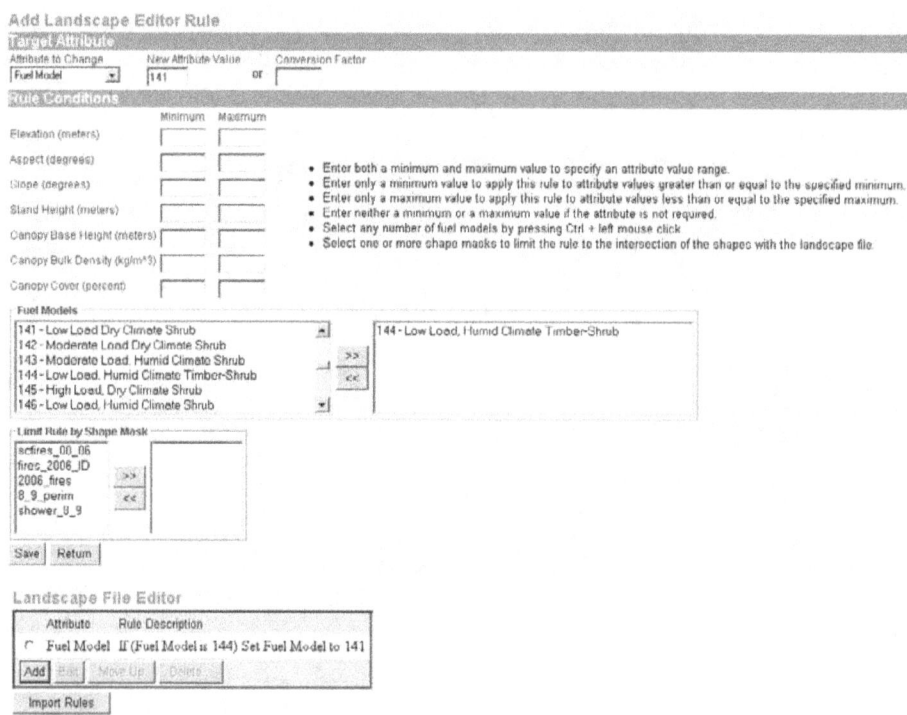

Figure 28. The landscape editor tool where a rule set was used to change fuel model 144 (SH4) to fuel model 141 (SH1).

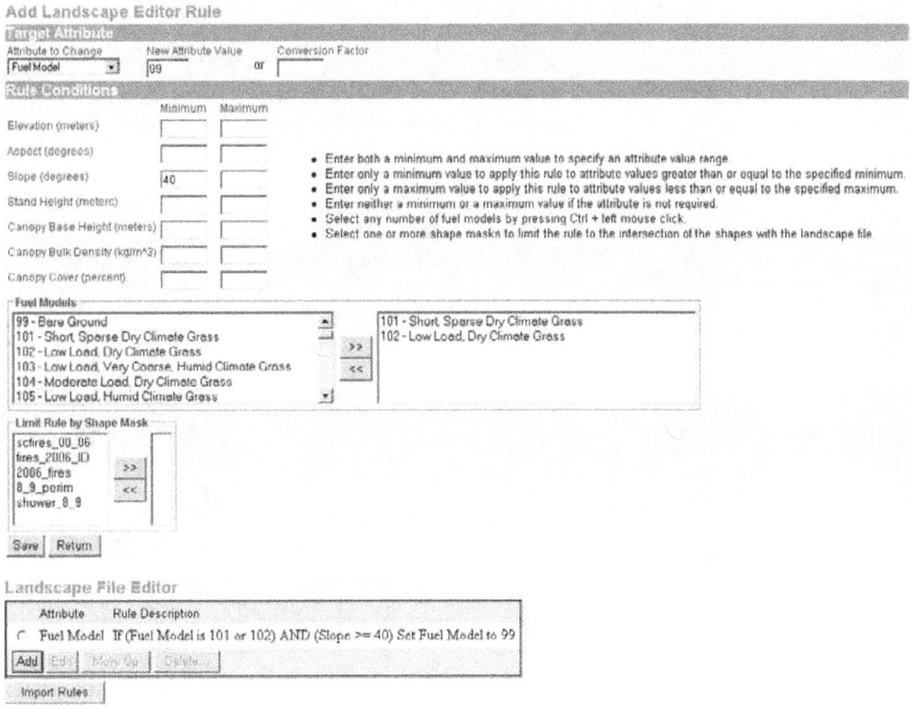

Figure 29. The landscape editor tool where a rule set was used to change all areas above 40° slope and fuel model 101 (GR1) and 102 (GR2) to fuel model 99 (NB9).

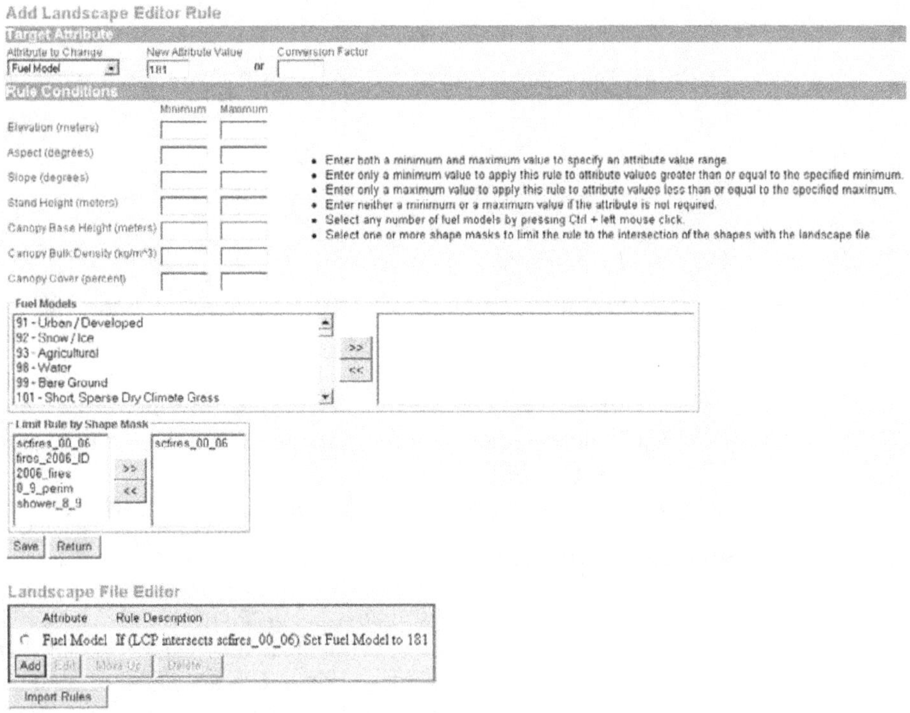

Figure 30. The landscape editor tool where a rule set and a mask were used to change recent fire areas to fuel model 181 (TL1).

USDA Forest Service Gen. Tech. Rep. RMRS-GTR-220. 2009

29

Reduction in Canopy Cover

Issue: A substantial portion of the LCP contained canopy cover in excess of 75%.

Resolution: From talking with local experts and reviewing published work in similar fuel types, canopy cover needed to be reduced by approximately 25% (fig. 31).

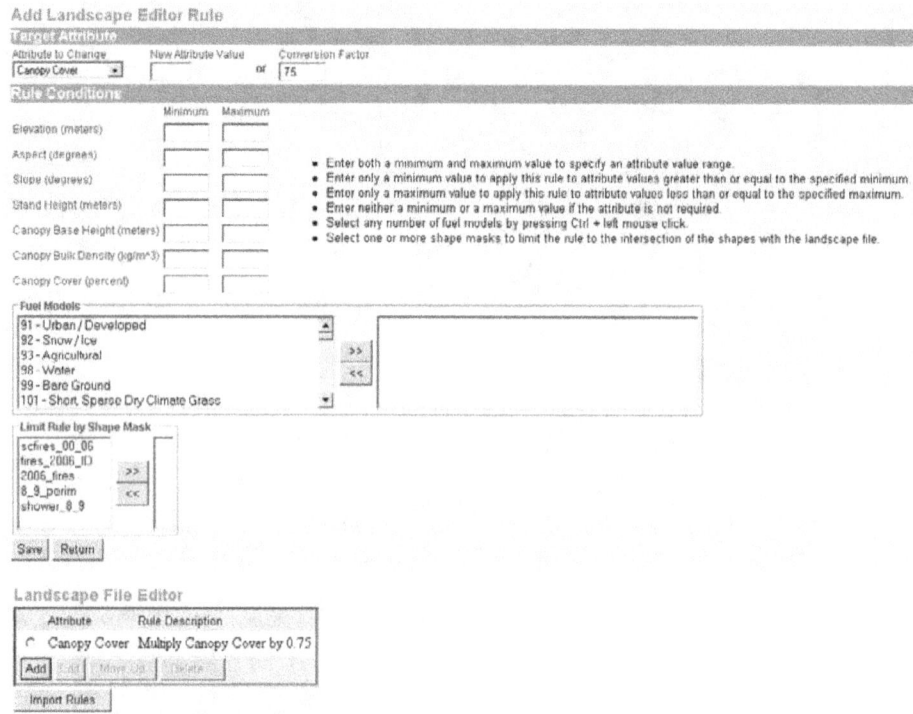

Figure 31. The landscape editor tool where a rule set was used to reduce canopy cover by 25%.

WFDSS Landscape Editor Tips

- There is no option for selecting numerical operators (e.g., +, /, -), so the value in the conversion factor is always multiplied.
- To use a mask – listed in the "limit rule by shape" box – the shapefile must be imported earlier (**Incidents** > **View Information** > **Shape Upload**).
- If multiple rules need to be applied to a layer, create one rule at a time, and an else statement will appear in the second rule.
- To select/deselect fuel models or masks use the Ctrl key and a left mouse click.

Making Complex Changes to the LCP

Occasionally, you will find significant problems with LANDFIRE data that can't be solved using the WFDSS editor (e.g., barren areas mapped as vegetation at various elevations and slopes). One can either refer the work to a GIS specialist or if he or she is familiar with GIS, they may be able to edit it using ArcMap or ArcView (refer back to Geospatial Critique, point eight). You may also want to consider the ACT (fig. 32) or the RCT (fig. 33).

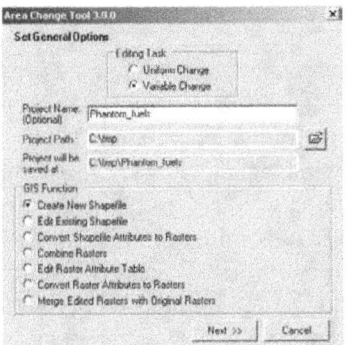

Figure 32. The Area Change Tool, showing the GIS functions available when the "Variable Change" editing task is selected.

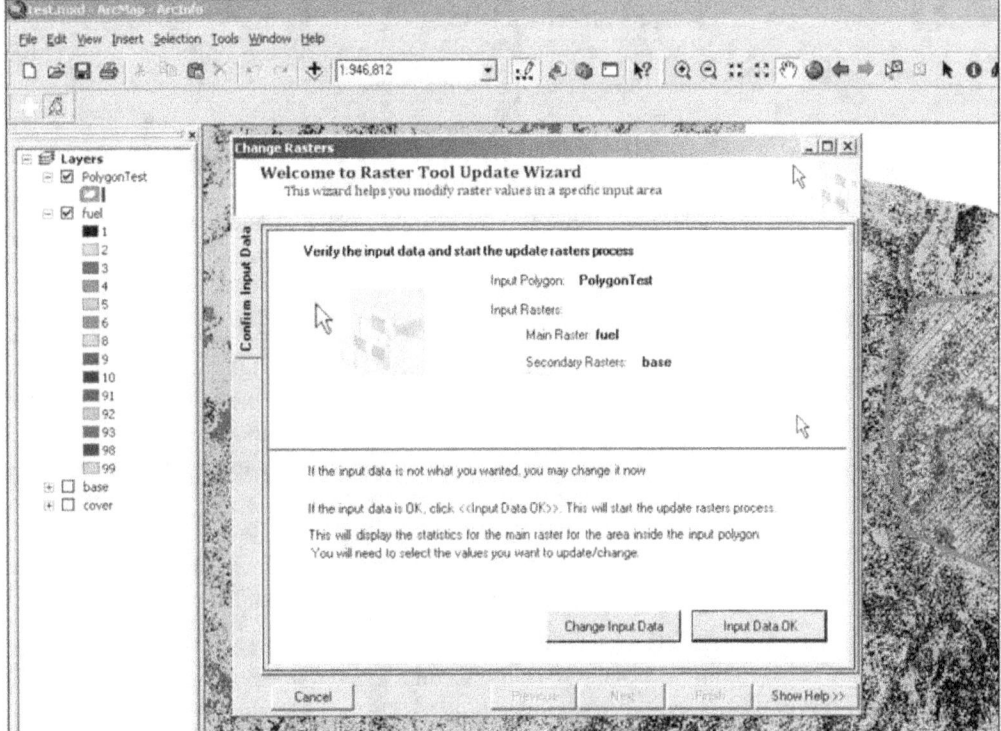

Figure 33. The Raster Change Tool Update Wizard.

ACT and RCT are ArcMap extensions specifically designed to edit raster fuels data, allowing users to perform complex GIS operations through a fairly easy interface. The ACT allows users to create, edit, convert, combine, and merge either vector or raster data. The ACT has a comprehensive user guide, tutorial, and program support via NIFTT (www.niftt. gov; click **Tools and User Documents**). The RCT is similar to the ACT, but has less vector functionality and is currently under development (that is, available for testing, but not for wide distribution) and support is limited (contact Craig Thompson [craig_thompson@nps. gov]). When widespread errors are found, it is important to bring these to the attention of the LANDFIRE development team (helpdesk@landfire.gov).

Geospatial Model Calibration

Calibration is critical to any landscape analysis. To produce fire growth and behavior outputs consistent with observations, model checking, modifications, and comparisons are done with known fire perimeters and weather conditions (Finney 2000). If the model has not been calibrated to local fires, analysts and managers will have less confidence in the output. On the other hand, when fire behavior outputs have been critiqued and the model calibrated adequately, one can have a higher degree of confidence in future simulations (Stratton 2006).

The term "calibration" is used freely in the wildland fire community. To truly calibrate something, you must have a similar standard to calibrate to. Furthermore, calibration is model specific. For example, we used MTT and a previous fire to critique ROS – a simple calibration exercise. However, it was of a short duration and environmental conditions were constant. Once you have updated the LCP, similar MTT exercises may prove beneficial as a quick calibration technique. Still, if time permits, a more robust approach is to use FARISTE. With FARSITE, you can calibrate to a longer duration fire, adjust spotting, and account for changes in weather, wind, and fuel moisture. The following information is adapted from Stratton 2006 and applies specifically to FARSITE, but most statements are applicable to MTT as well.

The fire perimeter is the most common fire behavior output calibrated. Where appropriate, calibration of fire type may be important for fire effects modeling and to accurately differentiate between surface fire spread rate (includes torching) and active crown fire spread. Field observations, still and video photography from aerial reconnaissance, and MTBS data can be used to calibrate fire type. Consider selecting one fire or run to calibrate the model under moderate conditions (prescribed fire), and another for extreme conditions (fig. 34) with and without a high wind event. *In order of importance*, criteria fundamental to any calibration exercise include:

- progression layer or detailed field observations that identify the position and time of the fire (e.g., field notes, dispatch logs), including a precise starting location;
- a fire of a sufficient size that includes several burn periods (>500 acres); ample and representative weather and wind information (e.g., RAWS(s) nearby);
- a fire that burned in several different fuel models and on varying terrain; accurate fuel moisture information;
- a fire with minimal suppression or knowledge of suppression tactics;
- a fire that burned under a variety of weather and wind conditions; and
- a fire that resulted in both surface and crown fire runs.

Sufficient calibration takes time and patience. Do not expect perfection given model assumptions and limitations, data inaccuracies, fire suppression, variability in the weather and wind, etc. Sometimes, FARSITE will adequately predict the shape of the fire, but not the timing of fire arrival. Every fire and LCP is different, hence every calibration exercise will vary. The following calibration tips usually hold true:

- Wind, weather, and fuel moisture files are crucial so enter inputs that are real as possible. Concentrating your time here will isolate several variables and streamline your calibration process. Make sure the station elevation is within the fire area and fuels are conditioned (if needed).
- Accurately define the burn period by the starting and ending time of daily fire movement.
- Select the appropriate model parameters – usually a coarser resolution at the start of your simulations, moving to a finer resolution as you get closer to completion.
- If spotting contributed to the growth of the fire, enable spot fire growth early on, but at a low frequency (0.5 to 1%). If fire spread is predominately through spotting, adjustments to CBH will likely be necessary.
- Make one modification at a time and then rerun the simulation.

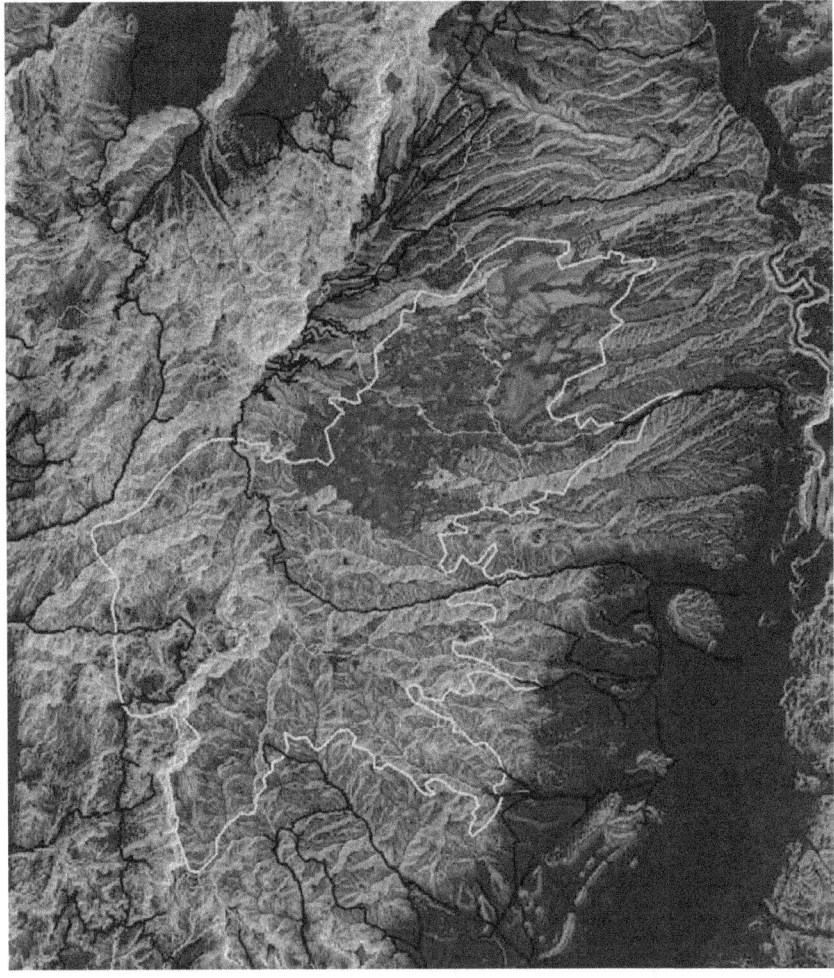

Figure 34. Calibration of the FARSITE model (in red; 16,686 acres) to a 3-day crown fire run on the northeast head of the Sanford Fire (June 2002; Panguitch, UT). Overlaid on slope are trails (green), roads (black), and the fire perimeter (blue).

- Do not try to calibrate the entire fire at once. Start with the first few hours or burn period and then build from there. If the initial progressions are off, it is likely the entire simulation will follow – a result of compounding error.
- For large fires, or where the origin or progressions are lacking, use a reliable perimeter and begin your calibration process there – watch for errors in perimeter dates and times.
- A substantial change (~0.3 to 0.4) in the adjustment file indicates a different fuel model may be needed. Try using a conversion file, or as a last resort, a custom fuel model.
- Adjust for the lack of extinction of the fire perimeter after nightfall or rain. This is important in light fuels, where the fire will resume once the fuel moisture drops (in reality that segment of the perimeter may be out).
- Personnel on the fire can be a useful resource as multiple perspectives lead to corroboration of key events.
- Keep a detailed log of model settings, parameters, adjustments, and outcomes throughout the calibration process.

USDA Forest Service Gen. Tech. Rep. RMRS-GTR-220. 2009

33

Maintenance and Documentation _____

Maintenance and documentation of geospatial fire data has always been a problem among federal and state agencies. Often the only time these data receive attention is when there is a need for decision support for a high-profile incident. Unfortunately, when the analysis or product is needed, the first few days of the incident are spent assembling the data, becoming familiar with the data, tracking down supporting documentation, and updating the layers. It is much easier to maintain landscape data than to let it slip into disrepair and be forced to update it under pressure. Sound fire management practices include geospatial data development, use, upkeep, and documentation. Indeed, fire specialists can use the data year round for prescribed fire and fuels planning, community wildfire protection plans (CWPP), National Environmental Policy Act (NEPA) compliance and documentation, wildfires, after action reviews (AAR), and outreach. Listed below are a few suggestions to improve documentation and maintenance of GIS fire data.

- Pull together two or three individuals with the responsibility of maintaining and documenting the GIS fire data. One person should be designated as the lead. These participants are likely those used to critique the LCP (i.e., the geospatial fuels team). They should meet every year and release an updated product in late winter or early spring.
- Assign specific responsibilities to group members (e.g., a fuels specialist makes a list of all landscape changes that need to be incorporated for that year).
- Keep an up-to-date list of items that need to be addressed by the next revision. It is easier to document these changes when the need arises than to try to recall them all later in the year.
- Before you make changes to the existing data, make sure there is a backup. When the data is updated, make sure there is a backup of that as well. External hard drives are great devices for sharing and backing up large amounts of data.
- With each change in the geospatial data, document the four W's: *What* change was made to the data, *who* did it, *when* was it done, and *why* was the data changed?

The Dilemma of Using LANDFIRE Fuels Data for Local Application

LANDFIRE fuels data is now available for the continental United States. Nationally, Rapid Refresh data will be used by Fire Program Analysis (FPA) for large fire growth simulation, and both Rapid Refresh and LANDFIRE National are available for use in WFDSS. It is convenient and useful to finally have seamless, current fuels data for landscape fire modeling. Although LANDFIRE fuels data were not designed for site-specific use, mid-scale or landscape-level application is usually possible and will see increasing use.

At present, updates to the LANDFIRE fuels data (e.g., Rapid Refresh) have been made from the top down, with periodic input from a handful of specialists via after action reviews, workshops, and personal communication. This procedure has produced a nationally consistent database that is adequate for regional and national planning, but local users often feel the product is inadequate for landscape fire and fuels application. The problem with this top-down approach is any edits made *at the local level* to LANDFIRE fuels data will not be incorporated nationally nor used by FPA or WFDSS. Indeed, there is little incentive to improve LANDFIRE fuels data locally because there is no systematic mechanism to incorporate local input. Until a compromise is reached (possibly in Refresh), local units can either (1) use the LANDFIRE data as is or (2) make modifications based on local data and expertise on a project by project or incident basis with the understanding that future updates of LANDFIRE fuels data are certain and local changes need to be documented for future application.

Summary

This paper was written to provide direction to fire specialists on LANDFIRE data acquisition, critique, and editing, as well as guidance on model calibration and discussion on data maintenance. This has been a challenging guidebook to write because many of the models and products are under development or in revision. Furthermore, a certain level of reader knowledge and tool competency was assumed to allow less specific instruction and more process and concept teaching. It is hoped, that if the procedure outlined in this paper is followed thoroughly, specialists' knowledge and capabilities will increase and their products will be improved leading to more informed decisions by line officers, incident commanders, and fire personnel.

References

Albini, F.A. 1979. Spot fire distance from burning trees: a predictive model. Gen. Tech. Rep. INT-56. Ogden, UT: U.S. Department of Agriculture, Forest Service, Intermountain Forest and Range Experiment Station. 73 p.

Alexander, M.E. 1988. Help with making crown fire hazard assessments. In: Fischer, W.C.; Arno, S.F., comps. Protecting people and homes from wildfire in the Interior West: Proceedings of the symposium and workshop; 1988 October 6-8; Missoula, MT. Gen. Tech. Rep. INT-251. Ogden, UT: U.S. Department of Agriculture, Forest Service, Intermountain Forest and Range Experiment Station: 147-156.

Anderson, H.E. 1982. Aids to determining fuel models for estimating fire behavior. Gen. Tech. Rep. INT-122. Ogden, UT: U.S. Department of Agriculture, Forest Service, Intermountain Forest and Range Experiment Station. 22 p.

Anderson, H.E. 1968. Sundance Fire: an analysis of fire phenomena. Res. Pap. INT-56. Ogden, UT: U.S. Department of Agriculture, Forest Service, Intermountain Forest and Range Experiment Station. 37 p.

Andrews, Patricia L. 2008. BehavePlus fire modeling system, version 4.0: variables. Gen. Tech. Rep. RMRS-GTR-213WWW. Fort Collins, CO: Department of Agriculture, Forest Service, Rocky Mountain Research Station. 107 p. http://www fs.fed.us/rm/pubs/rmrs_gtr213.pdf.

Andrews, P.L.; Bevins, C.D.; Seli, R.C. 2005. BehavePlus fire modeling system, version 3.0: user's guide. Gen. Tech. Rep. RMRS-GTR-106WWW. Ogden, UT: U.S. Department of Agriculture, Forest Service, Rocky Mountain Research Station. 142 p. http://www.fs fed.us/rm/pubs/rmrs_gtr106 html.

Andrews, P.L.; Rothermel, R.C. 1982. Charts for interpreting wildland fire behavior characteristics. Gen. Tech. Rep. INT-131. Ogden, UT: U.S. Department of Agriculture, Forest Service, Intermountain Forest and Range Experiment Station. 21 p.

Andrews, Patricia L. 1986. BEHAVE: fire behavior prediction and fuel modeling system-BURN Subsystem, part 1. Gen. Tech. Rep. INT-194. Ogden, UT: U.S. Department of Agriculture, Forest Service, Intermountain Research Station. 130 p.

Bahro, B.; Barber, K.H.; Sherlock, J.W.; Yasuda, D.A. 2007. Stewardship and fireshed assessment: a process for designing a landscape fuel treatment strategy restoring fire-adapted ecosystems: Proceedings of the 2005 national silviculture workshop. Gen. Tech. Rep. PSW-GTR-203. Albany, CA: U.S. Department of Agriculture, Forest Service, Pacific Southwest Research Station. p. 41-54.

Box, G.E.P. 1979. Robustness in the strategy of scientific model building. In: R.L. Launer and G.N. Wilkinson, Eds., Robustness in Statistics. Academic Press: New York.

Bradshaw, L.S.; McCormick, E. 2000. FireFamily Plus user's guide, version 2.0. Gen. Tech. Rep. RMRS-GTR-67WWW. Ogden, UT: U.S. Department of Agriculture, Forest Service, Rocky Mountain Research Station. http://www.fs fed.us/fire/planning/nist/ffp_v3_user_guide.pdfx

Burnham, K.P.; Anderson, D.R. 1998. Model selection and inference. New York: Springer.

Butler, B.W.; Forthofer, J.M.; Finney, M.A.; Bradshaw, L.S.; Stratton, R.D. 2004. High resolution wind direction and speed information for support of fire operations. In: Aguirre-Bravo, Celedonio, et al. eds. Monitoring science and technology symposium: unifying knowledge for sustainability in the Western hemisphere: Conference Proceedings. 20-24 September 2004; Denver, CO. Proceedings RMRS-P-42CD. Ogden, UT: U.S. Department of Agriculture, Forest Service, Rocky Mountain Research Station: 1-17.

USDA Forest Service Gen. Tech. Rep. RMRS-GTR-220. 2009

35

Butler, B.W.; Finney, M.; Bradshaw, L.; Forthofer, J.; McHugh, C.; Stratton, R.; Jimenez, D. 2006. WindWizard: A new tool for fire management decision support. In: Andrews, Patricia L.; Butler, Bret W., comps. Fuels Management – How to measure success: Conference Proceedings. 28-30 March 2006; Portland, OR. Proceedings RMRS-P-41. Fort Collins, CO: U.S. Department of Agriculture, Forest Service, Rocky Mountain Research Station: 787-796.

Byram, G.M. 1959. Combustion of forest fuels. In: K.P. Davis (ed.). Forest fire: control and use. McGraw-Hill Book Company, New York. p. 61-89.

Carlton, D.W. 2005. Fuels management analyst suite user guide. Fire Program Solutions/Acacia Services, Sandy, OR. 112 p.

Cruz M.G.; Alexander M.E.; Wakimoto R.H. 2003. Assessing canopy fuel stratum characteristics in crown fire prone fuel types of western North America. International Journal of Wildland Fire 12: 39-50.

McHugh, Charles W. 2006. Considerations in the use of models available for fuel treatment analysis. In: Andrews, Patricia L.; Butler, Bret W., comps. 2006. Fuels management-how to measure success: Conference Proceedings. 28-30 March 2006; Portland, OR. Proceedings RMRS-P-41. Fort Collins, CO: U.S. Department of Agriculture, Forest Service, Rocky Mountain Research Station: 81-105.

Finney, M.A. 1998. FARSITE: Fire Area Simulator-model development and evaluation. Res. Pap. RMRS-RP-4. Ogden, UT: U.S. Department of Agriculture, Forest Service, Rocky Mountain Research Station. 47 p.

Finney, M.A. 2000. A spatial analysis of fire behavior associated with forest blowdown in the Boundary Waters Canoe Area, Minnesota. Duluth, MN: U.S. Department of Agriculture, Superior National Forest. 121 p.

Finney, M.A. 2002. Fire growth using minimum travel time methods. Can. J. For. Res. 32(8):1420-1424.

Finney, M.A. 2006a. An overview of FlamMap fire modeling capabilities. In: Andrews, Patricia L.; Butler, Bret W., comps. 2006. Fuels management-how to measure success: Conference Proceedings. 28-30 March 2006; Portland, OR. Proceedings RMRS-P-41. Fort Collins, CO: U.S. Department of Agriculture, Forest Service, Rocky Mountain Research Station: 213-220.

Finney, M.A. 2006b. A computational method for optimizing fuel treatment locations. In: Andrews, Patricia L.; Butler, Bret W., comps. 2006. Fuels management-how to measure success: Conference Proceedings. 28-30 March 2006; Portland, OR. Proceedings RMRS-P-41. Fort Collins, CO: U.S. Department of Agriculture, Forest Service, Rocky Mountain Research Station: 107-124.

Finney, M.A. In prep. Fire spread probability. Missoula, MT: U.S. Forest Service, Rocky Mountain Research Station, Fire Sciences Laboratory.

Jennings, S.B.; Brown, N.D.; Sheil, D. 1999. Assessing forest canopies and understory illumination: canopy closure, canopy cover and other measures. Forestry 72(1):59-73.

National Interagency Fuels Technology Team. 2008. Area change tool user's guide for ArcMap 9.2, Version 3.0.0. 77 p.

Ottmar, Roger D.; Vihnanek, Robert E.; Wright, Clinton S. 2003. Stereo photo series for quantifying natural fuels in the Americas. In: Proceedings of the Second International Wildland Fire Ecology and Fire Management Congress and Fifth Symposium on Fire and Forest Meteorology, November 16-20, 2003, Orlando, FL. American Meteorological Society. P1.4 http://www.fs.fed.us/pnw/fera/publications/photo_series_pubs.shtml

Reinhardt, E.D.; Crookston, N.L. 2003. The fire and fuels extension to the forest vegetation simulator. Gen. Tech. Rep. RMRS-GTR-116. Fort Collins, CO: U.S. Department of Agriculture, Forest Service, Rocky Mountain Research Station. 209 p.

Reinhardt, E.; Lutes, D.; Scott, J. 2006. FuelCalc: a method for estimating fuel characteristics. In: Andrews, Patricia L.; Butler, Bret W., comps. 2006. Fuels management-how to measure success: Conference Proceedings. 28-30 March 2006; Portland, OR. Proceedings RMRS-P-41. Fort Collins, CO: U.S. Department of Agriculture, Forest Service, Rocky Mountain Research Station: 273-282.

Rothermel, R.C. 1972. A mathematical model for predicting fire spread in wildland fuels. Res. Pap. INT-115. Ogden, UT: U.S. Department of Agriculture, Forest Service, Intermountain Forest and Range Experiment Station. 40 p.

Rothermel, R.C. 1991. Predicting behavior and size of crown fires in the northern Rocky Mountains. Res. Pap. INT-438. Ogden, UT: U.S. Department of Agriculture, Forest Service, Intermountain Forest and Range Experiment Station. 46 p.

Roussopoulos, P.J.; Johnson, V.J. 1975. Help in making fuel management decisions. Research Paper NC-112. St. Paul, MN: U.S. Department of Agriculture, Forest Service, North Central Forest Experiment Station. 16 p.

Scott, J.H.; Reinhardt, E.D. 2001. Assessing crown fire potential by linking models of surface and crown fire behavior. Res. Pap. RMRS-RP-29. Fort Collins, CO: U.S. Department of Agriculture, Forest Service, Rocky Mountain Research Station. 59 p.

Scott, J.H.; Burgan, R.E. 2005. Standard fire behavior fuel models: a comprehensive set for use with Rothermel's surface fire spread model. Gen. Tech. Rep. RMRS-GTR-153. Fort Collins, CO: U.S. Department of Agriculture, Forest Service, Rocky Mountain Research Station. 72 p.

Scott, J.H.; Reinhardt, E.D. 2005. Stereo photo guide for estimating canopy fuel characteristics in conifer stands. Gen. Tech. Rep. RMRS-GTR-145. Fort Collins, CO: U. S. Department of Agriculture, Forest Service, Rocky Mountain Research Station. 49 p.

Scott, J.H. 2006. Comparison of crown fire modeling systems used in three fire management applications. Res. Pap. RMRS-RP-58. Fort Collins, CO: U.S. Department of Agriculture, Forest Service, Rocky Mountain Research Station. 25 p.

Stratton, R.D. 2004. Assessing the effectiveness of landscape fuel treatments on fire growth and behavior. Journal of Forestry, Oct.-Nov. 102(7): 32-40.

Stratton, R.D. 2006. Guidance on spatial wildland fire analysis: models, tools, and techniques. Gen. Tech. Rep. RMRS-GTR-183. Fort Collins, CO: U.S. Department of Agriculture, Forest Service, Rocky Mountain Research Station. 15 p.

Thomas, P.H. 1963. The size of flames from natural fires. In: Proceedings ninth symposium on combustion. Ithaca, NY: 844-859.

Thompson, C. In prep. Raster Change Tool. Boise, ID: U.S. Park Service, Fire Program Analysis System.

U.S. Geological Survey. 2000. Map projections. U.S. Department of the Interior. Reston, VA. www.usgs.gov.

U.S. Forest Service. 1996. KCFAST: Kansas City fire access software user's guide. Washington, DC: U.S. Department of Agriculture, Forest Service, Fire and Aviation Management.

Van Wagner, C.E. 1977. Conditions for the start and spread of a crown fire. Canadian Journal of Forest Research. 71(3): 23-34.

USDA Forest Service Gen. Tech. Rep. RMRS-GTR-220. 2009

37

Appendix A: Abbreviations and Acronyms _____

AAR	After action review
ACE	Acquire, critique, edit
ACT	Area Change Tool
AFMO	Assistant fire management officer
AMR	Appropriate management response
CBD	Canopy bulk density
CBH	Crown base height
CC	Canopy cover
CFA	Crown fire activity
CWPP	Community Wildfire Protection Plans
DEM	Digital elevation models
DOQ(Q)	Digital orthophoto quad or quarter quad (DOQQ)
DRG	Digital raster graph
ESRI	Environmental Research Institute
EVT	Existing vegetation type
FARSITE	Fire Area Simulator
FBAN	Fire behavior analyst
FFE	Fire and Fuels Extension to the Forest Vegetation Simulator
FIA	Forest Inventory and Analysis
FL or *L*	Flame length
FLI or *I*	Fireline intensity
FMC	Foliar moisture content
FMO	Fire management officer
FPA	Fire Program Analysis
FPU	Fire planning unit
FRAMES	Fire research and management exchange system
FSPro	Fire Spread Probability
FVS	Forest Vegetation Simulator
GIS	Geographic information system
GSTC	Geospatial Service and Technology Center
KCFAST	Kansas City Fire Access Software
LANDFIRE	Landscape fire and resource management planning tools project
LCP	Landscape file (used by FARSITE, FlamMap, and FSPro)
LFDAT	The LANDFIRE Data Access Tool
MODIS	Moderate Resolution Imaging Spectroradiometer
MTBS	Monitoring trends in burn severity
MTT	Minimum Travel Time
NEPA	National Environmental Policy Act
NIFTT	National Interagency Fuels Technology Team
NLCD	National Land Cover Data
NPS	National Park Service
PDF	Portable document format
RAWS	Remote Automated Weather Station
RCT	Raster Change Tool

RDDS	Rapid data delivery system
RMRS	Rocky Mountain Research Station
ROS	Rate of spread
RSAC	Remote Sensing Application Center
SEM	Systems for Environmental Management
SH	Stand height
SME	Subject matter experts
TOM	Treatment Optimization Model
USFS	U.S. Forest Service
USGS	United States Geological Survey
WFDSS	Wildland Fire Decision Support System
WRCC	Western Regional Climate Center

USDA Forest Service Gen. Tech. Rep. RMRS-GTR-220. 2009

39

Appendix B: Text Report From LCP Critique

The text report from LCP Critique contains the text distribution for *each* FARSITE theme, but for the purposes of this appendix only one fuel model distribution is provided (fuel model 165).

```
FlamMap Landscape File Critique
Landscape File: C:\1Dvs2D\BROOK.lcp
        Latitude: 45
        Cell Resolution X: 30.00      Cell Resolution Y: 30.00
        Num Cells East: 2341  Num Cells North: 2676
        UTM North: 4670444.000000
        UTM South: 4590194.000000
        UTM East: 35309.000000
        UTM West: -34891.000000

Themes present
        Theme             Units         Range
        --------------------------------------------------------
        Elevation         Meters        996 - 3172
        Slope             Degrees       0 - 71
        Aspect            Degrees       0 - 359
        Fuel              Class         91 - 189
        Canopy Cover      Percent       0 - 62
        Stand Height      Meters*10     0 - 375
        Base Height       Meters*10     0 - 35
        Bulk Density      kg/m^3*100    0 - 58


Elevation distribution
        Elevation             Frequency       Percent      Overall Percent
        -------------------------------------------------------------------
            996 -   1237         41043          0.66           0.66
           1237 -   1478        187047          2.99           2.99
           1478 -   1719        454072          7.25           7.25
           1719 -   1960        914520         14.60          14.60
           1960 -   2201       1414387         22.58          22.58
           2201 -   2442       1691602         27.00          27.00
           2442 -   2683       1243350         19.85          19.85
           2683 -   2924        307062          4.90           4.90
           2924 -   3165         11431          0.18           0.18
           3165 -   3406             2          0.00           0.00
           No Data                   0          0.00           0.00


Slope distribution
        Slope                 Frequency       Percent      Overall Percent
        -------------------------------------------------------------------
              0 -      7        179074          2.86           2.86
              7 -     14        564873          9.02           9.02
             14 -     21       1031708         16.47          16.47
             21 -     28       1738011         27.74          27.74
             28 -     35       1990551         31.78          31.78
             35 -     42        669238         10.68          10.68
             42 -     49         76759          1.23           1.23
             49 -     56         11653          0.19           0.19
             56 -     63          2287          0.04           0.04
             63 -     70           362          0.01           0.01
           No Data                   0          0.00           0.00
```

```
Aspect distribution
        Aspect                  Frequency      Percent      Overall Percent
        ---------------------------------------------------------------------
          0  -    36             629272         10.05           10.05
         36  -    72             593274          9.48            9.47
         72  -   108             625752          9.99            9.99
        108  -   144             685461         10.95           10.94
        144  -   180             671915         10.73           10.73
        180  -   216             601746          9.61            9.61
        216  -   252             520971          8.32            8.32
        252  -   288             549757          8.78            8.78
        288  -   324             690818         11.03           11.03
        324  -   360             692294         11.06           11.05
        No Data                    3256          0.05            0.05


Fuels distribution
        Fuel Type    Frequency      Percent      Overall Percent
        ---------------------------------------------------------------
          165        1479839        23.62           23.62
          184        1311822        20.94           20.94
          122        1163250        18.57           18.57
          183         964715        15.40           15.40
          189         607949         9.70            9.70
          102         298358         4.76            4.76
          142         191880         3.06            3.06
          121         102916         1.64            1.64
          101          60053         0.96            0.96
          188          57121         0.91            0.91
          144          16285         0.26            0.26
          146           6686         0.11            0.11
           92           1978         0.03            0.03
           93           1406         0.02            0.02
          161            256         0.00            0.00
           91              2         0.00            0.00
        No Data           0         0.00            0.00


Canopy Cover distribution
        Canopy Cover            Frequency      Percent      Overall Percent
        ---------------------------------------------------------------------
          0  -     0           2140331         34.17           34.17
         15  -    15                98          0.00            0.00
         25  -    25            198650          3.17            3.17
         35  -    35            313016          5.00            5.00
         42  -    42            717292         11.45           11.45
         45  -    45            461406          7.37            7.37
         49  -    49            704880         11.25           11.25
         55  -    55           1232570         19.68           19.68
         62  -    62            496273          7.92            7.92
        No Data                      0          0.00            0.00


Stand Height distribution
        Stand Height            Frequency      Percent      Overall Percent
        ---------------------------------------------------------------------
          0  -     0           2140331         34.17           34.17
         25  -    25              1183          0.02            0.02
         75  -    75               688          0.01            0.01
        175  -   175           4101154         65.47           65.47
        375  -   375             21160          0.34            0.34
        No Data                      0          0.00            0.00
```

USDA Forest Service Gen. Tech. Rep. RMRS-GTR-220. 2009

41

Crown Base Height distribution

Crown Base Height		Frequency	Percent	Overall Percent
0 -	3	2141753	34.19	34.19
3 -	6	4809	0.08	0.08
6 -	9	40754	0.65	0.65
9 -	12	551300	8.80	8.80
12 -	15	1174354	18.75	18.75
15 -	18	684287	10.92	10.92
18 -	21	289903	4.63	4.63
21 -	24	256962	4.10	4.10
24 -	27	328899	5.25	5.25
27 -	30	791495	12.63	12.63
No Data		0	0.00	0.00

Crown Bulk Density distribution

Crown Bulk Density		Frequency	Percent	Overall Percent
0 -	6	2473792	39.49	39.49
6 -	12	974130	15.55	15.55
12 -	18	1256258	20.05	20.05
18 -	24	1067919	17.05	17.05
24 -	30	419208	6.69	6.69
30 -	36	73008	1.17	1.17
36 -	42	144	0.00	0.00
42 -	48	43	0.00	0.00
48 -	54	13	0.00	0.00
54 -	60	1	0.00	0.00
No Data		0	0.00	0.00

Fuel Model Specific Distributions

```
*******************************************************************
```
Fuel Model 165
```
*******************************************************************
```
Elevation Range Distribution (Fuel Model 165, Meters)

Elevation		Frequency	Percent	Overall Percent
996 -	1237	546	0.04	0.04
1237 -	1478	7962	0.54	0.54
1478 -	1719	60441	4.08	4.08
1719 -	1960	214445	14.49	14.49
1960 -	2201	436555	29.50	29.50
2201 -	2442	513108	34.67	34.67
2442 -	2683	230794	15.60	15.60
2683 -	2924	15984	1.08	1.08
2924 -	3165	4	0.00	0.00
3165 -	3406	0	0.00	0.00
No Data		0	0.00	0.00

Avg (valid obs only): 2188.0 Overall Average: 2188.0

Slope Range Distribution (Fuel Model 165, Degrees)

Slope		Frequency	Percent	Overall Percent
0 -	7	31703	2.14	2.14
7 -	14	138580	9.36	9.36
14 -	21	295540	19.97	19.97
21 -	28	474901	32.09	32.09
28 -	35	426216	28.80	28.80
35 -	42	105797	7.15	7.15
42 -	49	6923	0.47	0.47
49 -	56	158	0.01	0.01
56 -	63	17	0.00	0.00
63 -	70	4	0.00	0.00
No Data		0	0.00	0.00

Avg (valid obs only): 24.0 Overall Average: 24.0

```
Aspect Range Distribution (Fuel Model 165, Degrees)
Aspect                  Frequency       Percent      Overall Percent
---------------------------------------------------------------------
     0 -      36         298627          20.18            20.18
    36 -      72         174683          11.80            11.80
    72 -     108          89940           6.08             6.08
   108 -     144          72613           4.91             4.91
   144 -     180          41281           2.79             2.79
   180 -     216          32215           2.18             2.18
   216 -     252          40081           2.71             2.71
   252 -     288          97372           6.58             6.58
   288 -     324         278914          18.85            18.85
   324 -     360         354068          23.93            23.93
   No Data                   45           0.00             0.00
---------------------------------------------------------------------
Avg (valid obs only): 193.6  Overall Average: 193.6

Canopy Cover Range Distribution (Fuel Model 165, Percent)
Canopy Cover            Frequency       Percent      Overall Percent
---------------------------------------------------------------------
     0 -       0              0           0.00             0.00
    15 -      15              0           0.00             0.00
    25 -      25              0           0.00             0.00
    35 -      35              0           0.00             0.00
    42 -      42              0           0.00             0.00
    45 -      45              0           0.00             0.00
    49 -      49         435376          29.42            29.42
    55 -      55         595164          40.22            40.22
    62 -      62         449299          30.36            30.36
   No Data                    0           0.00             0.00
---------------------------------------------------------------------
Avg (valid obs only): 55.4  Overall Average: 55.4

Stand Height Range Distribution (Fuel Model 165, Meters*10)
Stand Height            Frequency       Percent      Overall Percent
---------------------------------------------------------------------
     0 -       0              0           0.00             0.00
    25 -      25             15           0.00             0.00
    75 -      75              6           0.00             0.00
   175 -     175        1471314          99.42            99.42
   375 -     375           8504           0.57             0.57
   No Data                    0           0.00             0.00
---------------------------------------------------------------------
Avg (valid obs only): 176.1  Overall Average: 176.1

Crown Base Height Range Distribution (Fuel Model 165, Meters*10)
Crown Base Height       Frequency       Percent      Overall Percent
---------------------------------------------------------------------
     0 -       3            596           0.04             0.04
     3 -       6           2702           0.18             0.18
     6 -       9          21051           1.42             1.42
     9 -      12         272775          18.43            18.43
    12 -      15         418299          28.27            28.27
    15 -      18         208571          14.09            14.09
    18 -      21          93218           6.30             6.30
    21 -      24          89723           6.06             6.06
    24 -      27         135277           9.14             9.14
    27 -      30         237627          16.06            16.06
   No Data                    0           0.00             0.00
---------------------------------------------------------------------
Avg (valid obs only): 17.4  Overall Average: 17.4
```

```
Crown Bulk Density Range Distribution (Fuel Model 165, kg/m^3*100)
Crown Bulk Density      Frequency         Percent        Overall Percent
------------------------------------------------------------------------
        0 -      6           762           0.05              0.05
        6 -     12         19035           1.29              1.29
       12 -     18        264486          17.87             17.87
       18 -     24        735178          49.68             49.68
       24 -     30        392299          26.51             26.51
       30 -     36         67895           4.59              4.59
       36 -     42           130           0.01              0.01
       42 -     48            40           0.00              0.00
       48 -     54            13           0.00              0.00
       54 -     60             1           0.00              0.00
     No Data                   0           0.00              0.00
------------------------------------------------------------------------
Avg (valid obs only): 20.9  Overall Average: 20.9
```

Appendix C: PDF Report From LCP Critique _____

The PDF report from LCP Critique contains an image and a graphical distribution for *each* FARSITE theme, but for the purposes of this appendix only two theme value distributions are shown (fuel model 165 and 184).

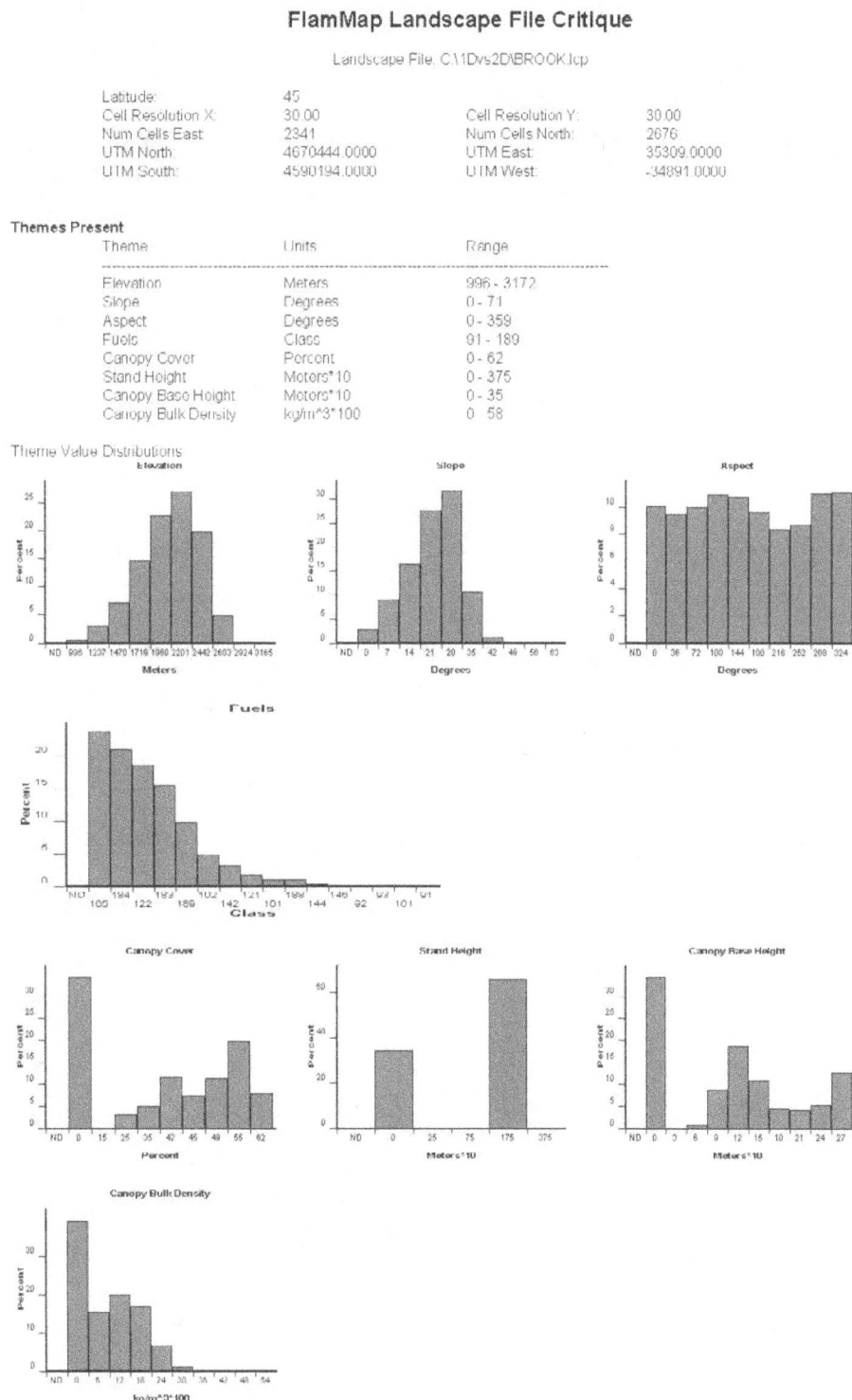

USDA Forest Service Gen. Tech. Rep. RMRS-GTR-220. 2009

45

Elevation

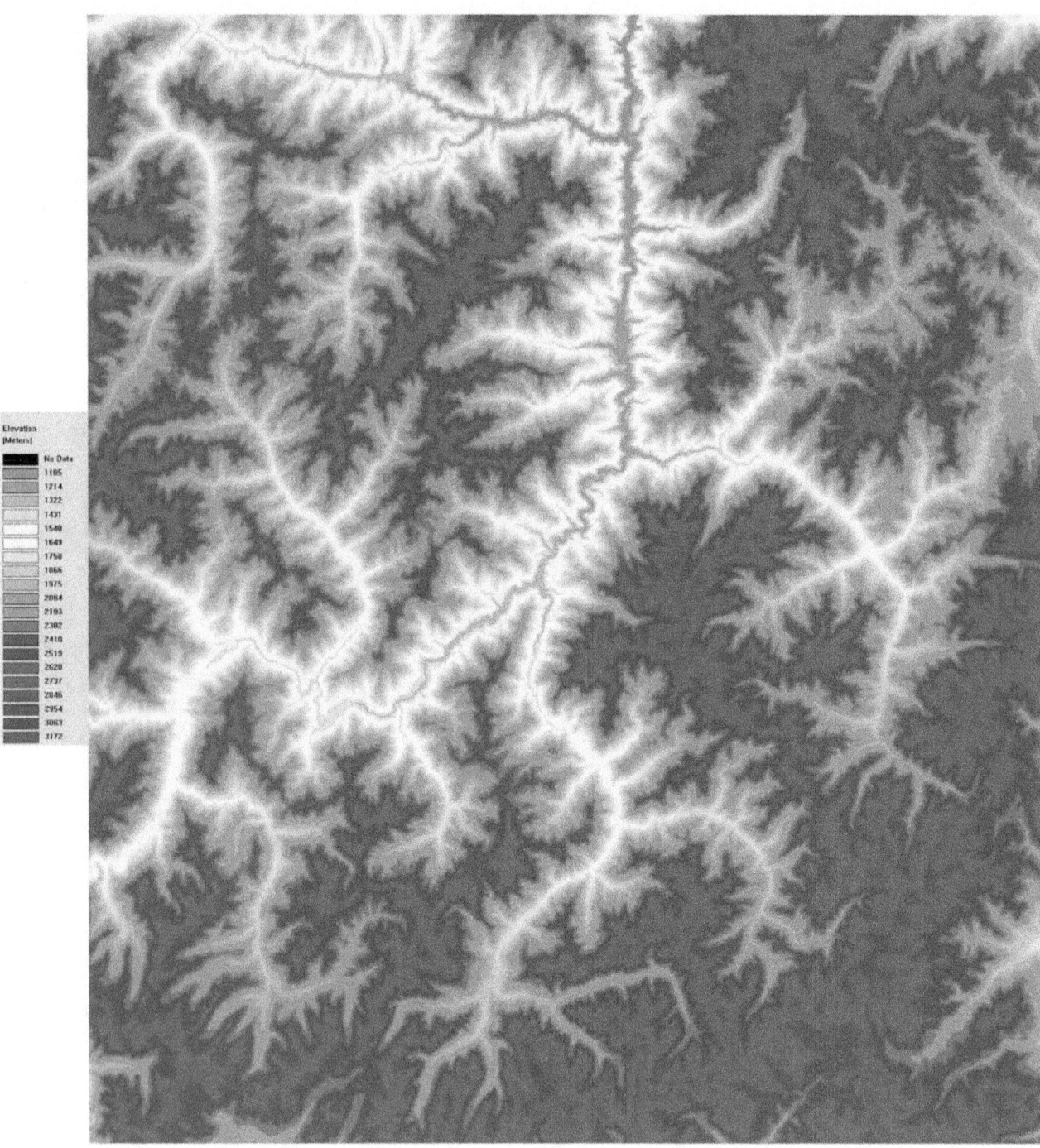

Slope

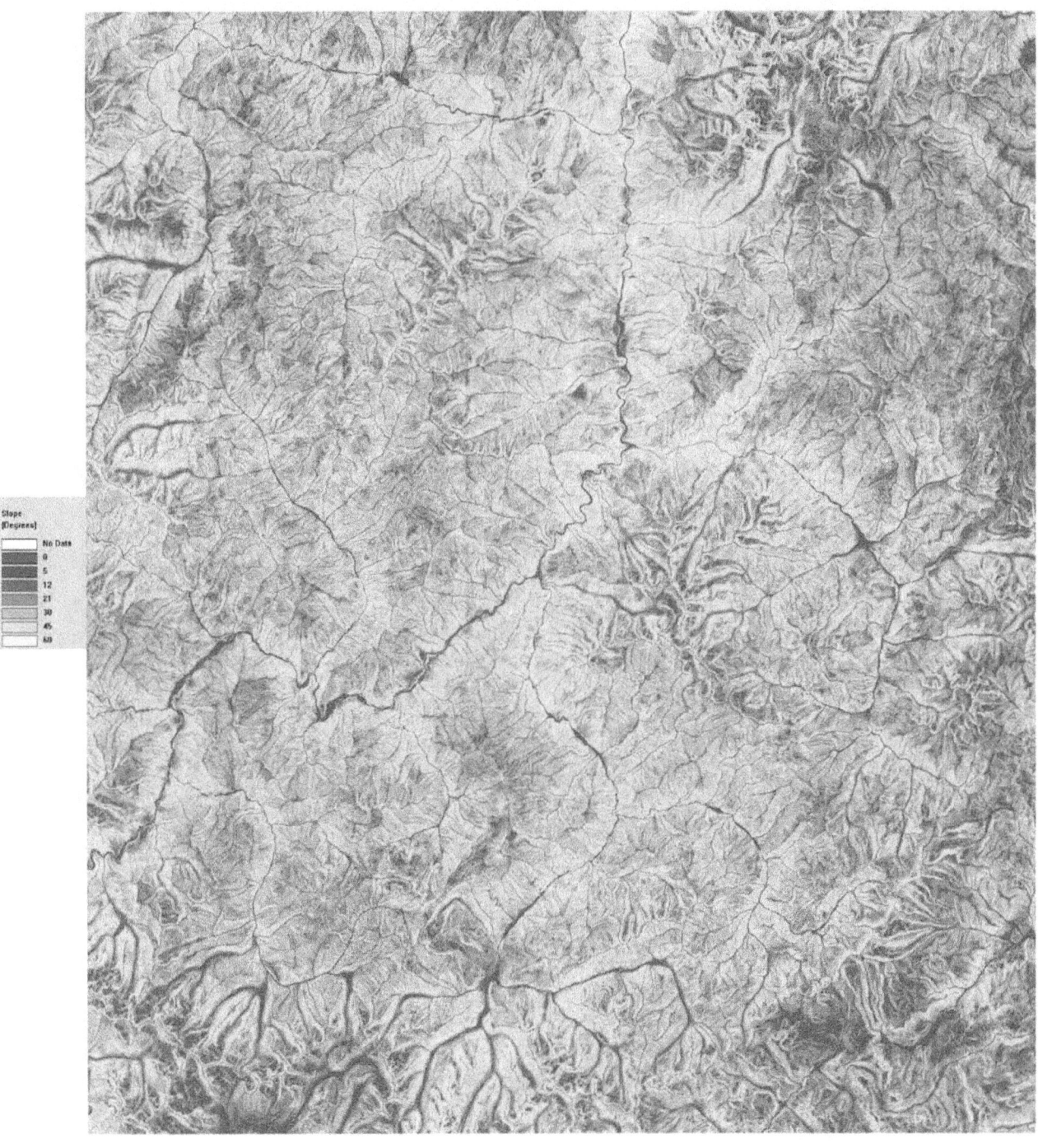

Slope
[Degrees]

	No Data
	0
	5
	12
	21
	30
	45
	60

USDA Forest Service Gen. Tech. Rep. RMRS-GTR-220. 2009

47

Aspect

48

4

USDA Forest Service Gen. Tech. Rep. RMRS-GTR-220. 2009

Fuels

USDA Forest Service Gen. Tech. Rep. RMRS-GTR-220. 2009

49

Canopy Cover

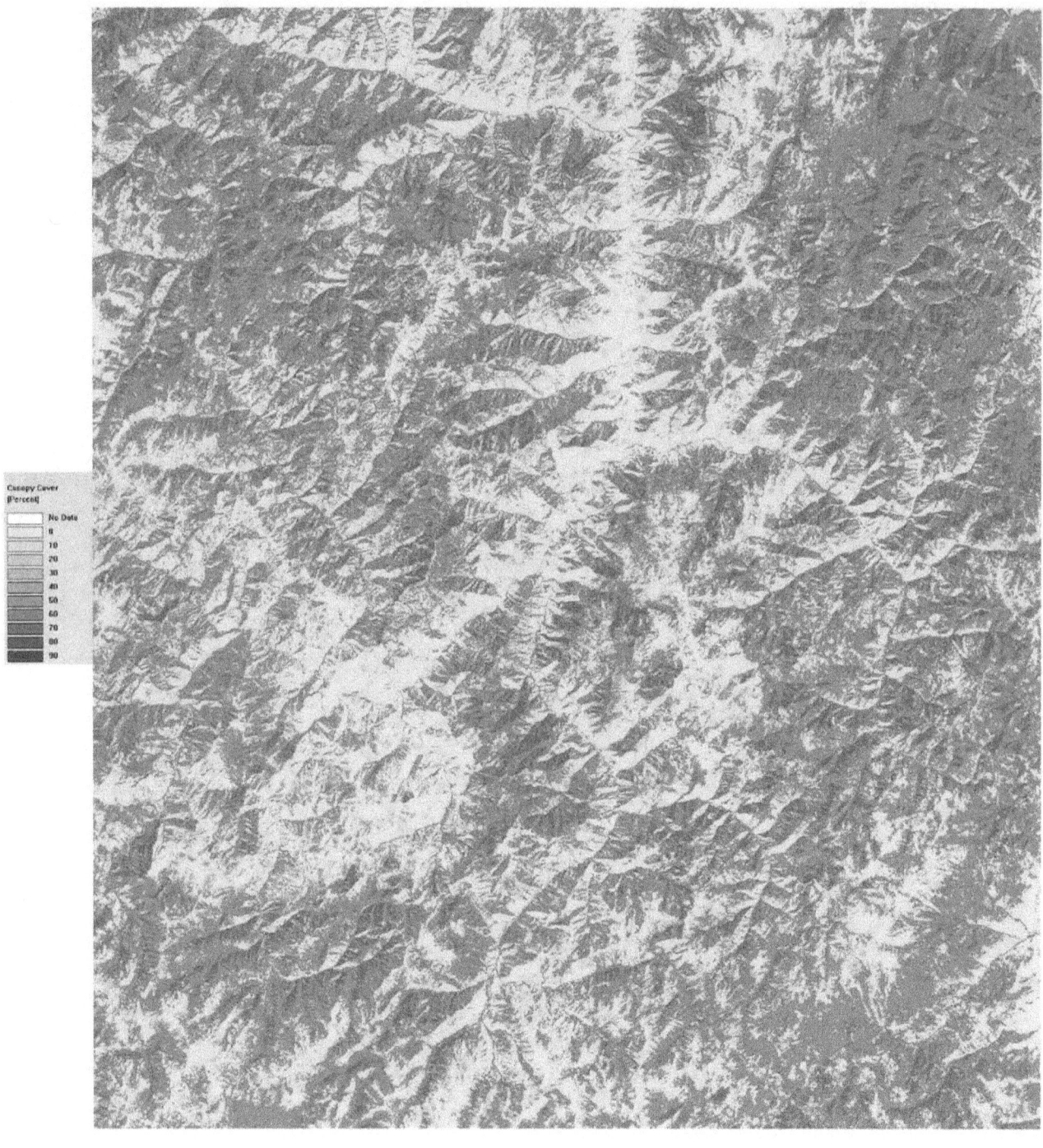

Stand Height

USDA Forest Service Gen. Tech. Rep. RMRS-GTR-220. 2009

51

Canopy Base Height

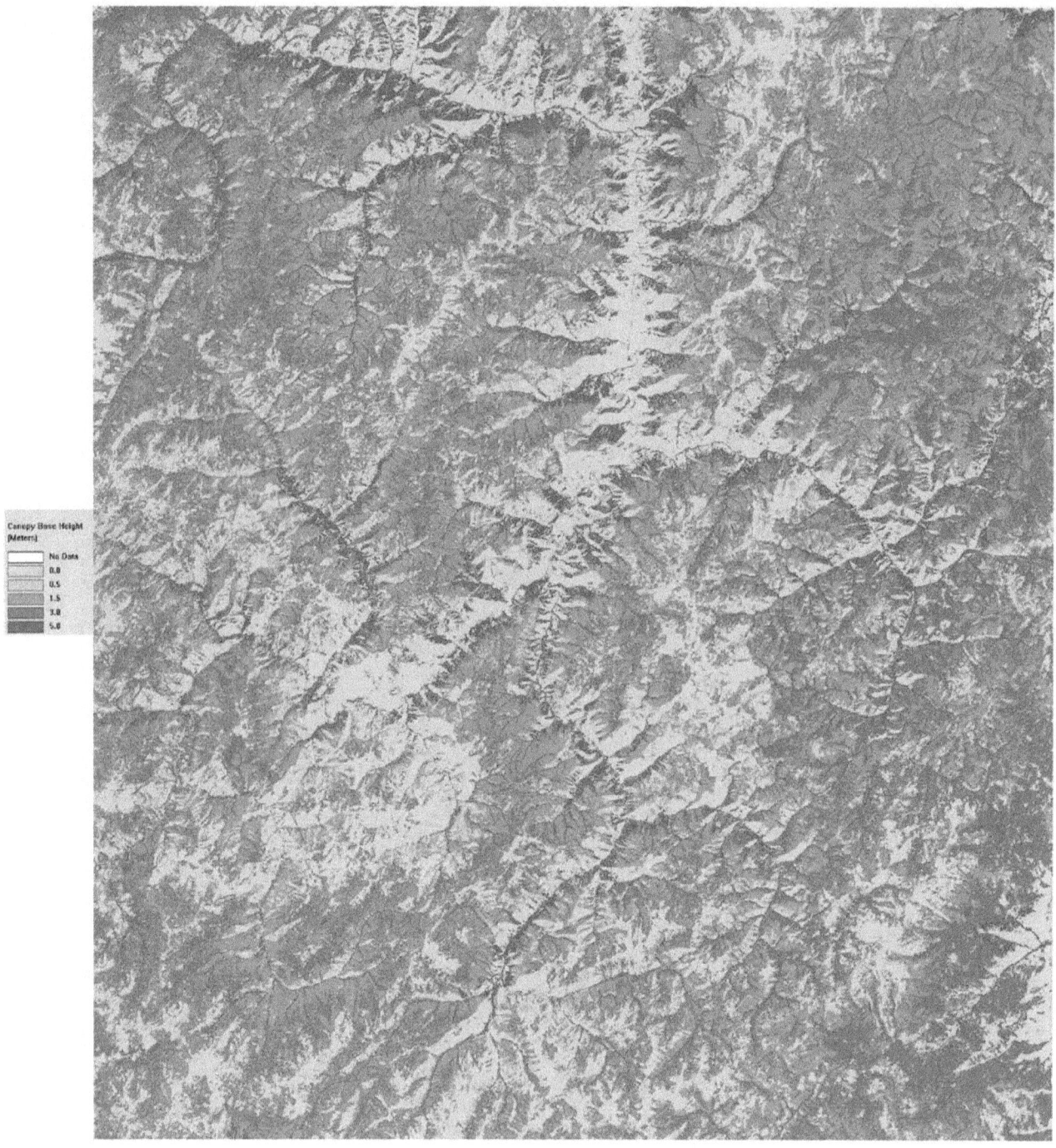

Canopy Bulk Density

Canopy Bulk Density
[kg/m^3]
- No Data
- 0.00
- 0.05
- 0.10
- 0.15
- 0.20
- 0.25
- 0.30
- 0.35
- 0.40

USDA Forest Service Gen. Tech. Rep. RMRS-GTR-220. 2009

53

Fuel Model 165 Theme Value Distributions

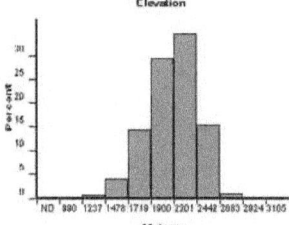

Elevation

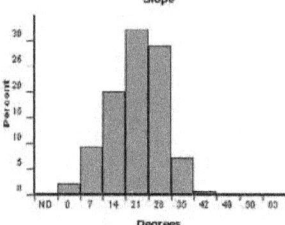

Slope

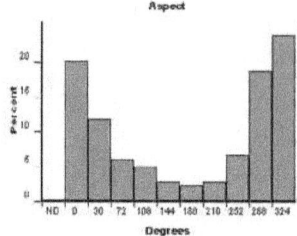

Aspect

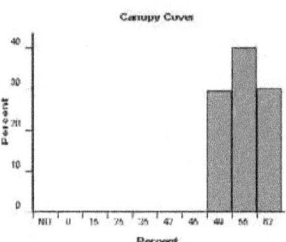

Canopy Cover

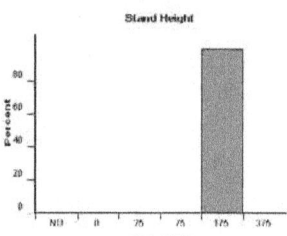

Stand Height

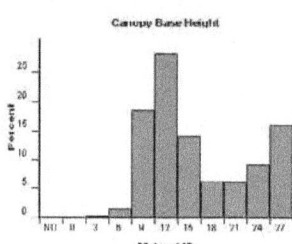

Canopy Base Height

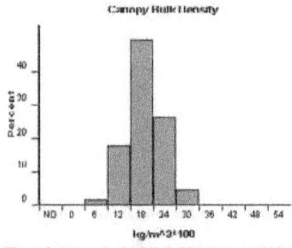

Canopy Bulk Density

Fuel Model 184 Theme Value Distributions

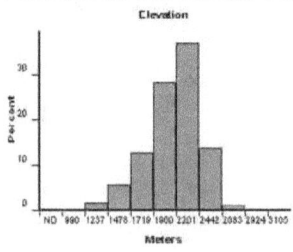

Elevation

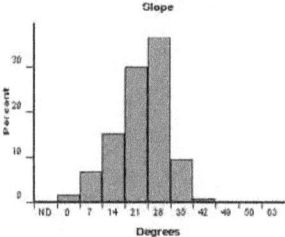

Slope

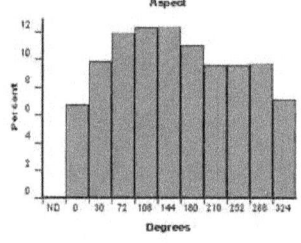

Aspect

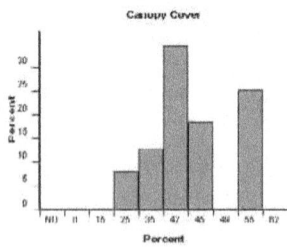

Canopy Cover

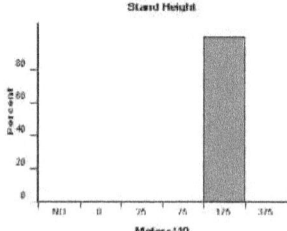

Stand Height

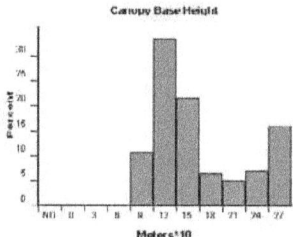

Canopy Base Height

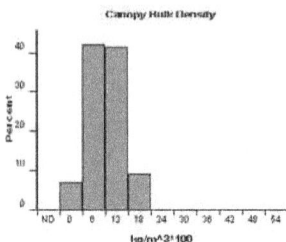

Canopy Bulk Density

10

54

USDA Forest Service Gen. Tech. Rep. RMRS-GTR-220. 2009

www.ingramcontent.com/pod-product-compliance
Lightning Source LLC
Chambersburg PA
CBHW081116280526
45787CB00007B/2855